ECONOMIST ON WALL STREET

Notes on the Sanctity of Gold, the Value of Money, the Security of Investments, and Other Delusions

Peter L. Bernstein

WILEY

John Wiley & Sons, Inc.

Published by John Wiley & Sons, Inc., Hoboken, New Jersey.
Published simultaneously in Canada.
Originally published by The Macmillan Company in 1970.

For general information on our other products and services or for technical support,
please contact our Customer Care Department within the United States at (800)
762-2974, outside the United States at (317) 572-3993 or fax (317) 572-4002.

Wiley also publishes its books in a variety of electronic formats. Some content that
appears in print may not be available in electronic books. For more information about
Wiley products, visit our web site at www.wiley.com.

Library of Congress Cataloging-in-Publication Data:

Bernstein, Peter L.
    Economist on Wall Street : notes on the sanctity of gold, the value of money, the
  security of investments, and other delusions / Peter L. Bernstein ; foreword
  by Arthur Levitt Jr.
        p.   cm.
    ISBN 978-0-470-28759-0 (pbk.)
        1. United States—Economic conditions—1961–1971.   2. Stock exchanges—
  United States.   I. Title.
  HC106.6.B46   2008
  330.973'0924—dc22

                                                                    2008028075

Printed in the United States of America
10 9 8 7 6 5 4 3 2 1

For
Robert L. Heilbroner

CONTENTS

New Foreword by Arthur Levitt Jr.   ix

Original Foreword by Gilbert E. Kaplan   xv

New Introduction   xxi

Original Introduction   xxxi

Chapter 1   Priorities Is . . .   1

Chapter 2   The Feel of the Market   8

Chapter 3   Inflation and the Economy   83

Chapter 4   Gold and the Balance of Payments   133

Chapter 5   How Wrong Can You Be?   174

Chapter 6   The Economist as Portfolio Manager   179

Chapter 7   Philosophy and Fantasy   225

Index   285

NEW FOREWORD

I have known Peter Bernstein, professionally and socially, for 35 years. Over that time the many and constantly changing sides of this remarkable person's intellect and personality have defied easy categorization. As anyone who has followed his career knows, Peter is brilliant, charming, and highly principled. Those of us who have worked closely with him also know him as an empathetic, proud, playful, and sometimes prickly person. Taken together, it's these traits that have anchored my own respect for him over our long and multifaceted relationship.

I first met Peter during the early 1970s when I was a partner in the brokerage firm called Carter, Berlind, Weill, and Levitt (CBWL). We were mostly a retail-oriented firm with a modest research presence, struggling to break into the institutional and investment banking space. I had heard of Peter at the time; he was a commanding presence on Wall Street—especially compared to our fledging enterprise. It would be a real coup for us if we could convince Peter and his firm to join with ours. Undaunted, I approached a friend, Hal Edelstein, who was an associate with Bernstein-Macaulay, about whether his small but well-regarded investment advisory firm would consider a relationship with CBWL. When Hal indicated interest in this suggestion, I immediately enlisted our senior partner, Arthur Carter, to join me in persuading Peter to merge Bernstein-Macaulay with our firm. We believed that Peter's personal stature, together with his firm's highly regarded clientele, would be an image-boosting move that might open institutional and high-end doors that might never have been accessible to our small firm.

Carter's charm and persistence won the day, and Bernstein-Macaulay became part of our enterprise, which over the years morphed into what is the Smith Barney brokerage arm of Citigroup. During the honeymoon period leading up to and following the merger, Peter displayed some of the traits I find to be frustrating and endearing. Over and over, Peter insisted upon the independence of Bernstein-Macaulay. His clients, mostly high-end professional and pension funds, must not become, as he put it, "dumping grounds for CBWL" underwritings, nor should they necessarily follow the investment recommendations of the CBWL analysts. His approach to the multiple levels of conflicts existing in the retail brokerage business was firm to the point of stubbornness. Peter's integrity was unimpeachable, and he helped set a tone for ethical behavior that, unfortunately, is hard to find in many Wall Street offices today.

As CBWL grew, Peter became a strong management presence—a wise and measured voice among a group of ambitious and often impetuous Wall Street wannabes. And as the two firms integrated, a deeply collegial relationship developed, and Peter started to accompany our brokers and analysts as they pitched for business. Over time, Peter became the centerpiece of many client conferences and dinners—and an invaluable part of our team. I remember clearly that as our firm started to grow, our investment bankers implored Peter to invest our clients' money in companies such as Tech AeroFoam, Arlen Properties, and Omega Alpha. "Conflict, conflict, conflict," muttered Peter to the frustration of our bankers and the benefit of his clients. On another occasion, Sandy Weill brought in a piece of business, the Topper Toy Company, that caught Peter's eye. In spite of Peter's and Sandy's analytic skills, they missed the improper accounting for toys that were booked as sales but returnable. This played out in a significant financial loss to a number of the firm's best clients and was a hit to the firm's reputation as well. To his credit, Peter blamed no one and accepted the responsibility for the kind of bad call that can plague almost everyone in the business of managing risks.

In addition to a towering intellect and superb analytic skills, Peter is at heart a people person. Quickly, he became the most respected and beloved partner of all his employees, and he used that personal touch to lighten the mood and close the deal.

For example, one of our firm's earliest partners, Clarence Jones, made an effort to attract banking business from a number of African and Caribbean nations, and Peter became the centerpiece of these pitches. One of the warmest memories of my career is recalling Peter—the scholarly and pixieish economist—going head-to-head with the Zambians to convince them to use the services of CBWL–Hayden Stone to underwrite their debt. On another occasion, we acquired our first branch in Beverly Hills from a failing firm, and had to move quickly to persuade the 12 brokers in the acquired office to stay with CBWL. Peter and I, plus our new branch manager, Herb Khaner, traveled west and regaled the new recruits with reasons they should join the team. They were interested, but then asked us to join them at a nightclub in the Valley. Little did we know that this was to be an evening of dancing, drinking, and general revelry. Without going into details, let me just report that Peter's good-natured participation sealed the deal.

Indeed, getting to know one's partners on a personal level is one of the benefits of a growing firm, and those relationships soon become part of the culture. Peter was a guest at our home, as my wife and I have been at his. Indeed, I'll never forget our first visit to his apartment near Sutton Place. I knew Peter as this former Williams College economics professor, rigorous with his data, serious about his commitment to his clients, and an astute businessman to boot. So imagine my surprise upon entering his apartment, when I saw two rabbits hopping around his home—a beautiful home decorated with a large collection of ceramic bunnies. From that moment on, Peter was the "bunny man" (although never within his earshot). And to me, that playfulness along with his brilliance are the parts of Peter's character that make him such an extraordinary human being, one I am privileged to call a friend.

—Arthur Levitt Jr.

ORIGINAL
FOREWORD

I suspect I first learned Peter Bernstein's approach to economics when he asked me to take care of his pet rabbit one summer a few years ago while he and his wife went on vacation. It was a chore I undertook with some trepidation, having had no previous experience in the care and feeding of rabbits. All I knew was that rabbits weren't supposed to make especially good house pets, being somewhat balky and not at all of the same devoted nature as dogs of my acquaintance. But Prospero, who was named aptly enough after Bernstein's first book, *The Price of Prosperity*, quickly made a convert of me; he soon began frolicking around like a playful pup and would sometimes even come running when I called his name. What was most revealing about this experience was that Bernstein had been unwilling to accept the widely held view that rabbits *had* to be unresponsive pets. This unwillingness to accept any point of view without extensive scrutiny is perhaps the cornerstone of his thinking.

It is probably typical of Peter Bernstein, moreover, that he would have a pet of such a rare and independent type. The fact is that Bernstein, whose iconoclastic writings you will be sampling in this volume, is a rare and independent man himself: rare in that he is one of the few people I know who is equally skillful as a practicing economist and as a professional investment manager of other people's money, and independent in that his philosophical approach is a constant questioning of what others have come to accept as conventional wisdom.

As you will see in the essays presented here, Bernstein's forte is scrutinizing what are generally believed to be basic truths, examining them in the light of empirical evidence and from that refreshing perspective coming to conclusions that would escape those with a less inquisitive frame of reference. This book, then, is the result of a continuing quest for economic knowledge—specifically in the area of the stock market.

Bernstein's provocative thought process seems to have been anticipated some decades ago by no less an economist than John Maynard Keynes, who is, by the way, quite obviously one of Bernstein's forebears. In his *General Theory*, Keynes described the process of professional investment and suggested that success in the field was akin to being able to pick the winner in a beauty contest. His point was that it was not enough to select the girl you yourself believe to be prettiest, nor, for that matter, the one you think the average opinion of the judges will pick as the prettiest. Rather, Keynes wrote, we have reached a third level, "where we devote our intelligences to anticipating what average opinion expects the average opinion to be."

It is on this third level that one begins to understand what is at the heart of Peter Bernstein's writings. Indeed, the fact that an idea or a belief is widely held in his view may very well *make* it suspect—or at least subject to rigorous questioning. The results of this probing have produced such work as his essays on the true role of gold in international monetary affairs, what government deficits really mean for prices, and how inflation influences stock prices over the long run—all of which are included in the pages following.

What to me is most striking about Bernstein's work, though, is his ability to bring clarity to even the most abstruse economic thinking. He has the ability to take a complex concept and make it simple, rendering it comprehensible to the lay reader and still interesting to the professional one. But unlike many others writing in the field, he shuns the emotional and visceral reaction and gravitates by instinct toward a rational and logical point of view.

To measure the extent of Bernstein's influence as a writer and an economist one need only look back to the days of the Kennedy Administration, an era when the government's fiscal responsibility to smooth out peaks and troughs in business activity—and the New Economics itself—had far less credibility than it does today. The biggest stumbling block to the tax cut the Administration had proposed was the United States Congress, and that legislative body, as so frequently happens, was something less than knowledgeable on the new direction economic policy was taking—specifically, the belief that a tax cut, contrary to the prevailing view, could be used to spur industry to new heights even in prosperous times. It thus fell to Bernstein and his longtime friend and fellow economist, Robert L. Heilbroner, to turn out a book that would explain the Administration's remedies to the public and, more important, to the Congress. The result was the immensely popular *A Primer on Government Spending*, produced after a series of marathon writing sessions starting at six o'clock in the morning, and published in a matter of weeks by Random House. Many believe this book, which was presented to every Senator and Congressman, helped to pave the way for the eventual passage of the tax-cut bill. The kind of analytical work it contained may be seen beginning on page 91, where the question of whether government deficits must necessarily lead to inflation is examined in detail.

This has been an age marked by the somewhat mystical quest for something called "investment performance"—a process by which one investment manager tries to outperform all others and tending to minimize personal relationships with clients. But through it all Bernstein's credo has remained a simple one. As he once told a reporter: "We feel our clients are people, not money, and the name of the game is their happiness." Underlying this personal view, one senses a strong social theory. The leitmotif running through his work is that the end result of economics and investment is that somehow people must be clothed and housed and fed. To accomplish this he has been an advocate of higher taxes, more government spending, and indeed, greater control of the economy by federal government. Not surprisingly, this approach has made Bernstein a bit of a maverick in Wall Street.

I have known Peter Bernstein as a student, employee, colleague, and friend over the past decade, the period during which most of the work in this book was being produced. I have learned an enormous amount from him over those years, and it is my hope that the readers of this book will find their exposure to Bernstein's thinking an equally enlightening experience.

—Gilbert E. Kaplan

NEW
INTRODUCTION

The origins of this book go back much farther than one might infer from looking at the contents. Its true origin was in 1934, or 36 years before its actual publication date. I was only 15 years old in 1934, but that was the year my father launched a new investment counsel firm called Bernstein-Macaulay, Inc. Macaulay was Frederick R. Macaulay, a distinguished academic in the process of writing a tome on the history of the bond markets.

My father's choice of starting out as an investment counselor instead of going into the brokerage business is interesting. Investment counseling was a young profession in those days, with only a handful of firms in the business. Indeed, most investors had never heard of it. Investment counselors render advice for a fee based on the size of the funds under management rather than in return for brokerage revenue. This arrangement, which is standard in the money management business today, has eliminated the long-standing conflict of interest that arises when an investor takes advice from a broker who makes money only when the client trades. A long-term, buy-and-hold kind of investor does little to fatten the pockets of his "customer's man" and is not likely to receive much attention. With a fee-based arrangement, activity plays no role in the advisor's compensation or in the nature and frequency of advice given. Indeed, for most of its existence, Bernstein-Macaulay was so sensitive to conflict of interest problems that it would not even recommend a broker to its clients.

Before going into the world of stock and bond markets, my father had managed a manufacturing business he had inherited from his father. In 1929, he received a buyout offer from a competitor at a price he never expected to see. He could not resist and sold out. As he described what happened next, he turned right around and invested the proceeds in the stock market at prices *nobody* had ever expected to see. He then invested his common stock holdings as his contribution to the partnership capital of a new brokerage firm he and a few friends were organizing. The firm had a short and not especially happy life. In 1933, when stock prices were about a third of what they were when my father had bought his stocks—and against his fervent objections—his partners chickened out. They insisted on liquidating the remaining assets of the firm, including my father's deeply depressed stock holdings.

A natural optimist and an unshakable believer in his own viewpoints, my father was convinced the market had already seen the bottom and that a great bull market lay ahead. In the spring of 1934, he borrowed $15,000 from a rich uncle and launched Bernstein-Macaulay, Inc., attracting as clients a few close friends who still had enough capital left to make the venture worthwhile. Stocks at that moment were about double the low of June 1932, and prices moved sideways for about a year. But then they took off.

The clientele grew, my father added associates to the firm who also brought in business, and he greatly enjoyed himself in the process. Part of the fun was writing a monthly letter, ostensibly to inform clients of the firm's views of the markets and the economy, but my father also hoped the letters would attract new clients. He had graduated from Harvard in 1902, and George Lyman Kittredge's course on Shakespeare had a lifelong influence on his enthusiasm for language, words, and literary style. The Bernstein-Macaulay letters were a wonderful opportunity for him to display and savor his talents as a writer. At home, the letters became known as "the release," and the word was not idly chosen.

My father died suddenly in 1951. At that time, I was working at a small commercial bank in New York, where I was involved in everything: lending money to small businesses, supervising the foreign department, and managing the securities portfolio. The work was enjoyable, my associates were good people and eager to advance my skills, and the pay was adequate. I had every indication I was launched on my lifetime career.

But when my father died and the future of Bernstein-Macaulay was at stake, my family put a lot of pressure on me to leave the bank and join my father's organization. They were convinced the firm would fall apart without my presence and my mother's financial security would be in danger. I was still reluctant—as I put it, I had no desire to become a social worker to the rich. But then my father's first client and best friend called me up and said he would without doubt remove his account unless I joined up. That clinched it and I gave in. That nice man subsequently became my stepfather and also introduced me to the wonderful woman I married in 1972, shortly after my first wife had died.

The prospect of writing the monthly Bernstein-Macaulay letters—the release—was an important element in my capitulation to the family pressures. Putting my views into good English was a joy I had inherited from my father. Writing had been a preoccupation at high school and college and has always been an vital part of my life (and my livelihood as well). I took over the task of writing the releases the very first month I was at Bernstein-Macaulay, although my older associate, Linhart Stearns, filled in on rare occasions. Linnie wrote one of the best and funniest issues ever, "A Modest Proposal," which appears here on page 273.

In those days, we referred to the letters more formally as "bulletins," as you will note throughout the book, but they were always "the release" in my heart and I have continued that form of reference to this very day in the letters we publish in the consulting firm I established when I finally left Bernstein-Macaulay in 1972.

The largest share of the material in this volume is composed of samples of the releases, but the book does contain a few articles written for outside publications. The most important of these, "Growth Companies versus Growth Stocks," was published in the *Harvard Business Review* in September 1956 and runs from pages 51 to 82. Although I had previously published two papers in scholarly journals, this article attracted a great deal of attention in Wall Street and established my reputation as a writer and an authority in the field of investing. After this, I was off and running.

The idea of buying a stock explicitly for its future earnings instead of its current earnings was a novel strategy in the 1950s, although growth stock investing came to dominate stock market investing in the 1960s and has played a vital role ever since. This type of investing involved paying a higher price than customary relative to current earnings and accepting a lower dividend yield as well. My article, original for its day, explained why this counterintuitive way of pricing stocks and valuing dividends was an acceptable approach to equity investing, and even preferable, under some conditions, to focusing on current earnings and seeking a high dividend return.

The range of material here is wide, from commentaries on current events in the capital markets and the economy to history of all sorts, a good deal of philosophy, and wide-ranging discussions of the outlook for inflation and the role of gold. Part of the fun of writing the releases was the opportunity to break away from the nitty-gritty of investing and explore more of the world around us. Those pieces consistently reflect the liberal views I held with such strong convictions at that time—and still do hold, although with convictions less absolute than in the old days. The best of these, in my view, are "Priorities Is . . ." (page 1) and "Is Work Necessary?" (page 238).

With the hindsight of more than 35 years, some of the current commentary and forecasts in the book look foolish. That is to be expected. We never know what the future holds and surely have not even a hint of what the world will look like 30-odd years ahead. But some of these releases looked foolish in the shorter run, say, within the next five years.

There was a common theme in those errors. At every opportunity, I am lighthearted about the threat of peace-time inflation. I believed with increasing conviction that the American economy's massive productive power, ingenuity, unmatched resources, competitive environment, robust financial strength, and appetite for risk taking would be able to deal with any adverse conditions that might arise. The extraordinary track record of stable or declining peacetime prices in the long history of our economy had repeatedly demonstrated how, under capitalism, supply overtakes demand and naturally keeps inflation in check.

This track record was violated only after my book was published. In the early 1970s Richard Nixon put through a huge increase in government spending to finance the war in Vietnam and persuaded the Federal Reserve to go lightly in restricting growth of the money supply—a process that nearly turned the United States into a banana republic and came to an end only after the redoubtable Paul Volcker assumed the chairmanship of the Fed in August 1979.

There is, finally, another common element running throughout the book, a view I still hold with the highest convictions. The objective of equity investing is survival. In the patois of today's professional investors, the objective of survival is just a straightforward way of saying that risk management is the secret of success. We have no control over what kinds of returns we will earn; we can only estimate, figure, and then hope. Risk is the key variable under our control.

Making a killing is a hope, not a strategy. The same goes for trying to beat the market. Taking risks so high that all can be lost is a strategy, but it is not the strategy I would choose. In the long run, equity investing has to be a positive-sum game or the capitalist economy will grind to a bitter end. That may, indeed, come about, but then a strategy built on the objective of survival is all the more important. If the outcome is the happier one, and the system does endure, time will bring sufficient reward to justify the forbearance that the survival strategy demands.

Looking back at the material in this book after the passage of nearly 40 years, do I find myself wiser today? Are there passages here I wish I had not written? If I had it to do over again, would I say it differently?

To answer the latter questions first, I admit there is one expression in this book I wish I could have eliminated. There is a superfluity of "of course" throughout the text. It is an expression I have come to detest. "Of course such-and-such is the case" conveys the snobbish message that readers are expected to know all about such-and-such but are so stupid they need this reminder from an author who is smarter and better informed than they are. I bridle every time I encounter it as a reader and am ashamed to have used with such abandon in the texts in this book.

The more interesting and difficult questions are whether I find myself wiser and whether I would say things differently were I to have the chance to rewrite these documents. I think all investors should find themselves wiser over time, because experience is a teacher—and there probably is no better teacher in the field of investing.

Unfortunately, experience can also lead you astray, so it has to be used with discretion, as I indicate just shortly.

In any case, there was nothing else but experience to go on when I started off as an investment counselor. The readings I did were all superficial, with the exception of Benjamin Graham.* Furthermore, there was no theory of investing to guide us. We built the practice of investing on folklore, rules of thumb, and the experience of older associates (which served me badly, because my older associates were grizzled veterans of the Great Crash and could not accept the postwar bull market's vitality and staying power).

But theory matters. I have learned a lot about the theory of investing since 1970, and that knowledge might have been helpful in analyzing some of the problems I tackled here. In fact, I have written two books about the theory of investment, published in 1992 and 2007, and have read and listened to more theoretical material than I care to remember. Theory introduces a discipline and orderliness in thinking that experience can seldom provide. I do think about some of these problems differently as a result of what theory has taught me.

---

*I am tempted to include Gerald Loeb's *The Battle for Investment Survival*, because, by suggesting a high-risk equity portfolio as a small proportion of total wealth and cash or its equivalent for the rest, Loeb implicitly put risk control into the center of decision making. I recall being deeply impressed with this book on first reading.

But the theoretical work carried out between 1952 and 1972 by eight Nobel Prize winners and their associates was not even beginning to attract the attention of practitioners in the late 1960s. I did not know it even existed. Perhaps the material in the book would have been richer if the theoretical material had been available to practitioners like me—but I suspect the subject matter of my writings and even the course of events would also have been different if the abstractions of the theoretical work had captured our interest. As a result, my writings would have covered other kinds of topics and answered other kinds of questions. So the issue is moot.

ORIGINAL
INTRODUCTION

People in Wall Street spend an inordinate amount of time telling one another things that are wrong, that the listener has heard already, and that he will soon be repeating to someone else. But if all the myths and homilies of the conventional wisdom were true, wouldn't all of us be rich?

Some of us are, but most of us are not. That is because the money game is a lot tougher to win than the advertisements, the market letters, and the friendly telephone calls would lead us to believe.

Of course, orthodoxy, particularly when it is embellished by constant repetition, is almost always reassuring to the person who hears it. When one deals constantly with the unknown and when every decision means taking another risk, the warm familiarity of what one has heard before (even if it is wrong) provides an urgently needed sense of security. The unknown is frightening enough: Why exacerbate matters by listening to the unfamiliar and radical ideas that someone else may put forth?

But the hard truth is that investment success comes most generously to those who are able to swim upstream; *majority opinion is already reflected in the current level of security prices.* Hence, the essays in this book represent an effort to cut through the heavy sludge of received doctrine, to test, and occasionally to ridicule, the things that most people spend most of their time telling one another about the economy, the stock market, and the art of portfolio management.

I am, in fact, continually amazed by the refusal of human beings to see what is right in front of their eyes on those occasions when what they see contradicts what they believe to be true. Thus, they believe that inflation is a time to take money out of the savings bank and to buy stocks, when, instead, stocks tend to go down during inflationary periods and to go up when prices are stable. They worship the golden calf, when, instead, gold has been about the worst investment that anyone could have made over the past 20 or 30 years. They look at business and businessmen as the foundations of our society, when, at every turn, these foundations show signs of crumbling and are at the very least held up to the most searching inquiry by the young and the radicals.

I am amused—and aggravated—above all by the repeated questioning on the part of prospective clients as to the rate of return they can "reasonably expect" from their investments in the future, as though the stock market were an accommodation machine that will provide them with whatever level of affluence they seek. These people simply refuse to believe that the future is always unknown to all of us. Yet, the art of successful investing begins with the humility of facing up to the unknown.

Hence, the common thread that runs through the essays in this book is the conviction that the future is not going to be where the other fellow tells you that you will find it; more likely, you should be striking out in quite a different direction.

Of course, we would be fools to run against the crowd all the time, and contrary thinking for its own sake is more a neurotic than a constructive activity. But the investor who blindly follows majority predictions and standard forecasts usually ends up in the ditch. My purpose here, in fact, is to show that the process of thinking with one's ears closed, difficult as it may be, is the only reliable path to profit.

I therefore urge the reader to pay some attention to the dates of publication of the various essays that follow, all of which appeared between 1955 and 1970. Most of them set forth controversial minority opinions at the time they were printed—and, in retrospect, I find that, the lonelier I felt in the positions I took, the more accurate my forecasts turned out to be.

Most of the selections are monthly bulletins that I wrote for the clients and friends of my investment-counsel firm, Bernstein-Macaulay, Inc.; space limitations forced me to be as concise and to the point as possible in the articulation of my opinions in these particular pieces. The balance of the essays is articles or speeches prepared over the same span of 15 years or so. I have preceded each major grouping of essays with an introduction, describing the major ideas expressed and occasionally helping the reader to understand the historical setting of something that was written in the past; where appropriate, I have written a postscript—"What Happened Afterward"—to individual pieces, so that the reader will have some sense of the accuracy of the predictions made. One section, in fact, is designed to show how wrong one can be in this game of trying to guess the future.

In this connection, I stress once again that these essays should be read with one eye on the date of publication. The topicality of what they have to say seems to bear surprisingly little relation to the amount of time that has passed since I wrote them.

Although the selections in each chapter appear in rough chronological progression, I have not hesitated to place something out of that order if that would give it added interest or help the sequence of argument.

I want to express my thanks to Herbert Nagourny, who originally suggested the format for this book, and

Original Introduction

to Mrs. Arthur Nolan, for endlessly patient and accurate assistance in preparing it for publication. My wife's enthusiasm and encouragement were essential; the dedication to my friend is an acknowledgment of a sense of gratitude that surpasses the possibilities of verbal expression.

ECONOMIST
ON
WALL STREET

Chapter 1

PRIORITIES IS . . .*

A fourteen-year-old boy died apparently of an overdose of pills yesterday, only hours after the Board of Education said it had no funds for security guards to fight narcotics problems at the school he attended. . . . Mayor Lindsay said, "This is a regrettable tragedy and I will ask for a full report on the incident from the Police Commissioner."

—*New York Times*, February 17, 1970

P riorities is when you have reports instead of money to save human lives. Priorities is when you have a boom in office building downtown and urban decay uptown. Priorities is when we grumble about paying higher rates for electricity and simultaneously grumble about air pollution from the local utility. Priorities

---

* A Bernstein–Macaulay bulletin, March 1, 1970.

is when we can afford to drop bombs on houses in Vietnam and can't find the financing to build houses at home. Priorities is when we cut back on appropriations for education and ask for extra appropriations for antiballistic missiles. Priorities is when you can take a walk on the moon but are afraid to walk down your own street. Priorities is when the Governor won't ask for higher taxes in an election year and then there is no money to provide a cheap and efficient public transportation service. Priorities is when we are willing to spend money to buy television sets to sit home and see thoughtful programs about the problems of our society that we don't want to spend any money to do anything about.

"Priorities" has been a cool word in the past. Today—and for many days to come—it will be the hottest word in our vocabulary.

For much of our history, including most years since the end of World War II, the American economy has operated with a margin of idle capacity and unemployed workers, so that increased demands from one area or another could be met with relatively little difficulty. Guns *and* butter was the cry. We could even have guns and butter and road-building and schools for a good deal of the time.

But now, as we look ahead into a new decade, the grammar is changing. For all the "and's" read "or." Affluent as we may be, the needs of our cities and our educational systems and our starved supply of housing and our defense establishment and our aspirations for more leisure and our burgeoning supply of 20- to 30-year-olds add up to astronomical numbers that even our fabulously productive economy cannot meet.

This means we will have to make some important choices. *To a greater extent than most people realize, however, we have already locked ourselves into some crucially important choices.* This will make the significance of selecting priorities even greater than it might have been otherwise.

To begin at the beginning: the direction in which we are moving and the largest of the deficiencies we are trying to overcome are all enormously *capital-using*. In other words, they require a large investment in labor and resources for a long period of time before they begin to bear fruit in quantity. Urban renewal, housing, education, public transportation, the drive against pollution, hospital building, and doctor training, to name just a few of the things we are in a hurry to accomplish, will absorb massive amounts of resources and will show results only gradually.

Furthermore, all of them require *financing*. Few of us have the ready cash to pay for a home without a mortgage, and the federal and local governments must have more tax revenues or borrow more money if they are to increase their expenditures. At the same time, as a result of the drastic drain on corporate liquidity in recent years, even moderate rates of business expansion now require high levels of external financing. In short, the urgent needs of our society imply intense pressures on our capital markets. This comes at a time when we are already absorbing a colossal volume of financing and when our usually efficient capital markets are groaning under the strain.

Since the external financing requirements of business are likely to remain high, since the unsatisfied demand for mortgages is enormous and growing daily, since state and local governments will have a clear need for tremendous sums, since the appetite of our defense establishment seems to be insatiable, and since major domestic federal programs are clamoring for attention, the probability is that we will have neither the real nor the financial resources to accomplish everything that we would like to accomplish.

Now there is one way to do it. Although business has insufficient cash flow to finance its expansion internally and although state and local governments are hard pressed to cover their expenditures right now, we could solve a lot of problems if the federal government could operate at a surplus. This would have a double advantage: The federal government would make no claims on the capital markets and, in fact, would be repaying debt out of the budget surplus and therefore putting money back into the coffers of the individual and institutional investors who buy the securities that businesses and local governments offer for sale. This is something of an oversimplication, because it depends to some extent on who pays the taxes, but the general concept is valid nevertheless.

If the federal government is to operate at a surplus and hence both relieve and replenish the capital markets, that means that revenues must exceed outlays. Which way are we to do it? By increasing revenues or by restraining expenditures? The degree to which the federal government can fulfill its share of improving the quality of life in the United States depends precisely upon this choice.

The problem is that the choice has already been made. The haste to remove the Johnson tax surcharge and the ultimate implications of the tax reform bill of 1969 both mean that the revenues of the federal government in the years ahead will be many billions of dollars less than they would have been if the choice had been made the other way. But this also means that the level of federal *spending* is going to be many billions of dollars less than it would have been otherwise. The only other choice is to persist in the disruption of our capital markets, to squeeze housing still further—or to revert to some type of credit control and rationing.

It is possible, perhaps even likely, that state and local governments will tax away the federal tax savings that Congress voted us last year and will therefore be able to fund some programs that might otherwise have been carried out on the federal level. Some people would even welcome a shift of responsibilities along these lines, and it does have certain attractions. However, it has two serious disadvantages. First, the citizens who end up paying higher state and local taxes may not be the same ones who get the full benefit of the federal tax savings. Second, the revenue-raising abilities of the states vary enormously: the rich states can improve themselves rapidly while the poorer states fall further behind. When projects are financed by the federal government, we can manage things in a more equitable fashion.

But we had best face up to the implications of what Congress has decided for us: The priority of our private pocketbooks is more important than the priority of our public needs. The federal government is going to have to count its pennies with great care. The question is not guns or butter, but guns or schools (and for "schools" you can read the whole array of urgent domestic programs).

How large a defense establishment can we *afford*? No question is more important today for our social and economic well-being. Note, the question is not: how large a defense establishment do we *want*? We have set up our priorities in such a way that we simply cannot have everything we might like the federal government to give us. We have to make the choice, no matter how difficult, now and in no uncertain terms.

The disarmament negotiations with the Soviets, the decisions with respect to Southeast Asia, the ABM controversy, and the fascination with new weapons systems are important not only in terms of what America's role in the world should be and in terms of judgments concerning the intentions of other great powers; we are simply unable to make decisions in the foreign policy area without simultaneously making decisions that determine the rate of fulfillment of domestic needs.

That is why, for the first time since the period of disillusionment after World War I, the military is on the defensive in the halls of Congress and before the public. In view of the rapidly changing age-structure of our population, they are likely to remain on the defensive for a long time to come. And here is the crucial point: At more than any other time in our history, the fate of our economy is going to be determined by the view we take of our society and our sense of social priorities.

Here is one hopeful note on which to end this dissertation. From 1948 to 1969, the average increase in the Standard & Poor's 500-stock index was more than three times as great during years in which defense expenditures were flat or declining as during years in which defense expenditures were rising. Excluding 1960 and 1961, when the usual relationship was reversed, the ratio was better than five to one in favor of years of flat or declining defense expenditures. Well, anyway, here's hoping!

Chapter 2

THE FEEL OF
THE MARKET

This group of essays consists essentially of current comment on what was happening in the stock market at the time they were written. Most current comment turns stale pretty fast, and much of the material I have turned out over the years would hardly qualify for a book of this sort. These pieces, however, do have some lasting relevance to what is happening today and to what is likely to happen tomorrow, because they draw attention to factors that most people were ignoring at the time. They represent hard efforts to predict the future in some kind of systematic fashion.

The first essay is concerned with Senator Fulbright's hearings on the stock market in early 1955. Although at that time the Standard & Poor's industrial average was 38 (it was to break up through 50 within 12 months and to double within seven years), and although volume was then running at only 2.5 million shares a day on the average, many people were worried about excessive speculation and overpriced securities. The ghost of 1929 was clearly still with us in 1955; the focus of attention was on the past to such an excessive degree that few people had any real awareness of the great bull market that still lay ahead. This piece is worth reading as a reminder of how we can be so much a victim of the current environment and of the past that we can seldom, if ever, guess the future.

The belief that one can predict the future persists among all of us. The short pieces that follow the comment on the Fulbright hearings show how a sense of perspective on the present can sharpen our ability to foresee what the future holds for us. For example, the two articles on institutional investors drew attention to trends that were then only beginning to emerge and that have subsequently become primary factors in the security markets. "The Anatomy of the Bear" presents a technique for determining when bear markets are likely to touch bottom: This particular piece called the turn right on the button. I was lucky enough to repeat this feat in the spring of 1968, in the item entitled "The Gold Crisis and the Security Markets," which was written just days before President Johnson's famous television address of March 31—and almost seems to predict his whole speech. The market took off like a shot immediately afterward. Ever since I was retained by the New York Stock Exchange in 1959 to project long-run volume trends, I have been fascinated by the possibilities for market forecasting revealed by the patterns of trading activity; two of the essays explore this area in some detail.

The article on growth stocks appeared in the *Harvard Business Review* in 1956. I would hardly pick the same names to exemplify growth stocks today, although I turned out to be on the right track when I rejected the oils and the steels as growth stocks at the time—a position that was then close to heresy. Nevertheless, the concept still seems valid; a growth company is, like the entrepreneur in Schumpeter's *Theory of Business Enterprise*, an inner-directed organism, capable of determining its own destiny through the creation of its own markets. The rather crude attempt to develop a new valuation formula for companies of this type was subsequently taken up by others, whose approach has been more sophisticated but whose basic concepts were identical with mine.

THE FULBRIGHT HEARINGS: A BLESSING IN DISGUISE?*

"One thing is apparent," said Mr. Funston, president of the New York Stock Exchange, on the day the Fulbright hearings came to a close. "The need for public education to protect the public against emotional and uninformed actions is even greater than we thought."

---

* A Bernstein–Macaulay bulletin, April 1, 1955.

The Feel of the Market

If there is any lesson to be learned from the Fulbright hearings, Mr. Funston has hit the nail on the head. It was not that the hearings themselves were such a circus (although Senator Fulbright's emphasis on opinions rather than facts was not too helpful), but that the reactions of the public, the stock market, the newspapers, and the Administration were keyed to an astonishingly emotional pitch.

But after one has cut through the emotionalism, the hearings were far from a waste of time, and a dispassionate and objective analysis of what happened can be helpful to the intelligent investor.

If one is willing to read beyond the headlines and give some study to what the experts *really* had to say, there was actually quite a bit of meat in the testimony. Among other things, the hearings indicated the following four observations:

1. The stock market has risen sufficiently high and at a steep enough pace to cause considerable concern among many observers who are less "controversial" than Professor John Kenneth Galbraith. Professor Graham, General Wood, and Messrs. Eberstadt, McCloy, Eccles, Livingston, and Martin all expressed doubts about the present level of the market. (All those who are called upon to express an opinion about whether the market is high or low will be everlastingly grateful to Winthrop Smith of Merrill Lynch, who made it pleasantly respectable to say, "I don't know!")

2. An increase in margin requirements is very unlikely until the market rises substantially above its March highs.

3. While the capital-gains tax presents its problems, revising the law on capital gains presents equally insoluble problems. Result: the chances are that nothing will be done about it.

4. Dishonest practices and rigging à la 1929 seem to be reassuringly conspicuous by their absence, and no new major legislation in this direction is necessary. Self-discipline and policing of trading and exchange activities (including "tipping") have been admirable except in cases where relatively small amounts of money are involved.

It would be interesting to know how many people bothered to find out what Professor Galbraith actually had to say. Certainly if one relied upon Senator Capehart's intense reaction to get the drift of the professor's remarks, one would think he had announced that Armageddon was just around the corner.

The fact of the matter is that Professor Galbraith has been writing a book about the fascinating year of 1929; an article in *Harper's* magazine this summer was based upon it (and somehow failed to knock the Dow Jones Industrial Average down 20 points), and so was his testimony at the Fulbright hearings. He devoted almost all of his testimony to a scholarly and highly interesting dissertation on the history and nature of speculation and how it was illustrated by what happened in 1929. He did *not* predict that the stock market was about to fall out of bed, and he did *not* predict that we face a major depression. *Indeed, he went to considerable length to point out how much sounder and more promising our present position is than the condition which existed in 1929.* Finally, he did *not* recommend an immediate establishment of 100 percent margin requirements; rather, he suggested the desirability of this move, "should there be a resumption of the upward movement of the past year in the weeks or months ahead."

The main purpose of Professor Galbraith's testimony was to provide perspective through an analysis of the nature of speculative excess and to describe the disastrous consequences that can follow from it; he urged the committee to remember that an ounce of prevention is worth a pound of cure, and, indeed, the following paragraph from his testimony is uncomfortably reminiscent of attitudes widely prevalent last November and December:

> What becomes important is the single fact that prices are rising. Because they are rising and money can be made, more and more people are encouraged to try and get a share in the capital gains. By doing so they keep prices going up. The original cause of the price rise eventually becomes the merest excuse for optimism. People use it—the promise of a New Era, the superior qualities of Florida sunshine, a sound and conservative or middle-of-the-road Administration—but only to

explain the capital gains they are making or hoping to make. . . . Equanimity, it will be evident, is the endemic disease of the boom. . . . One result is that any suggestion that values are unreal—that things are less than wonderful—is fiercely resisted.

Professor Galbraith's prediction of "fierce resistance" was made on March 8, and in the days that followed, the chairman of the Republican National Committee, the Secretary of Commerce, the Secretary of the Treasury, and the President himself all rose to the bait, acting almost as if they had sustained a personal insult. Treasury Secretary George M. Humphrey's statement was both the most important and the most intelligent, and although he said, "I gave up years ago trying to figure out the stock market," we should still take note of the following argument:

As criticisms of the Government and suggestions for restrictive actions have been made from day to day before the Committee and in the public press, and with the discussion of restrictive action that the Government might or might not engage in, [the hearings] can easily contribute to a questioning of confidence and uncertainty as to what the future might hold.

A few days later, these sentiments were echoed by Mr. Fairless of U. S. Steel, when he observed,

I do not see any danger [of a collapse] and I am not forecasting [*sic*]. My old mother used to tell me that a good thing to do when you don't want to get into trouble is to stop talking about it. I think that time has arrived.

With due respect to our able Secretary of the Treasury and to the elderly Mrs. Fairless (who was probably thinking of something quite different from the stock market), these pleas to stop public discussion of the state of the economy and of the stock market are simply appalling. Can the fabric of confidence really be so fragile? *Are we allowed to discuss freely what the government might do if the Communists attack Quemoy but forbidden to discuss what it might do if the Dow Jones Industrials attack 450?* Are we to become a nation of Candides, convinced that all is for the best in the best of all possible worlds, because the doubting Thomases, rightly or wrongly, are to be throttled? Can any thinking American citizen, be he bear or bull, subscribe to such a philosophy without flinching?

For reasons which we confess we have never understood, the Administration apparently believes that their most important vote of confidence must be registered at the corner of Broad and Wall streets in New York rather than at the corner of Main Street in every community of the country. Instead of taking their cue from the persistently rising level of consumer spending and the impressive stability of business expenditure on plant and equipment, they are unusually sensitive to fluctuations on the stock market.

And yet it is time that they realize (as Mr. Hoover did before 1929, but failed to express strongly enough) that they face their greatest dangers from a stock market that floats up into a stratosphere divorced from economic realities, for from markets such as those come the truly disastrous crashes that do destroy confidence. Every investor should be joined by the Administration in welcoming any setback, no matter how sharp, which squeezes out the speculators and reminds us that the market is not a one-way street. Only in that way can we be sure that the madness of 1929 will not be repeated.

A SHORT WALK THROUGH THE LONG RUN*

We all know people who become restless with a stock if it fails to show a profit within weeks or even days after they buy it. Others are so convinced of the immutability of the stock market's long-term uptrend that investing to them consists of nothing more than buying good stocks and holding on indefinitely, paying no heed to whatever interruptions may come along. Indeed, some investors are so convinced of the unshakable momentum of the uptrend

---

* A Bernstein–Macaulay bulletin, March 1, 1966.

that they ask us repeatedly what size gain they can "reasonably expect" over the next year or five years or ten.

Yet is was not always thus, as we may see from the chart on page 18, showing the course of industrial common-stock prices from 1871 to 1965. The uptrend is there, all right, clearly defined. But two facts are clear at once:

1. The uptrend during the 78 years prior to 1949 was a much more labored affair than it has been during the 16 years since 1949. In the 11 downturns before World War II, but excluding 1929, an average of 56 months had to pass before the old high was regained; since 1949, the old highs have always been regained within 15 months at the most.

2. The postwar bull market far outshadows anything in our history. Prices have risen at an average annual rate of 12.6 percent since 1949, more than quadruple the rate of growth from 1871 to 1949.

Thus, if prewar patterns had prevailed since 1949, prices today might still be around their 1929 highs and we would not yet have fully recovered from the 1962 market break.

On many occasions in the past, investors must have found the long pull hard going indeed and muttered, as Lord Keynes once did, "In the long run, we are all dead." Only 16 years have passed since 1949, but the periods 1847–1897, 1915–1933, and 1925–1942, all longer than 16 years,

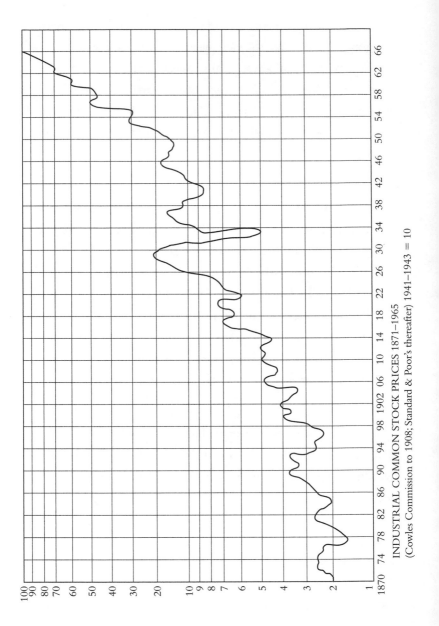

INDUSTRIAL COMMON STOCK PRICES 1871–1965

(Cowles Commission to 1908; Standard & Poor's thereafter) 1941–1943 = 10

18

began and ended with prices at identical levels. The investor who bought in 1929 would have had to wait more than 20 years to see daylight; by 1965 he would have shown a relatively unexciting annual increment of only 4.5 percent. During the 26 long years from 1871 to 1897, the market fluctuated but no uptrend is apparent at all.

Draw a line touching the lows of 1884, 1908, 1919, 1942. This clearly defines the long-term uptrend. Now extend that line out to 1965, where it hits 16 (even the steeper uptrend touching 1908, 1914, 1918, 1949 only reaches 25 in 1965). This shows that prices could fall 75 percent to 80 percent from their present lofty level *and still leave the basic upward pattern intact!*

One consolation to all of this is that both the magnitude and the quality of corporate earning power have greatly improved since prewar days. The character of common-stock ownership, in part because of the long, steep upswing, has also undergone a fundamental transformation. Yet no one who looks at this perspective of the great bull market and has any respect for history can afford to ignore what he sees.

What Happened Afterward:

The Standard & Poor's stock average over the next three and a half years never rose much more than about 10 percent over the March 1966 level; during the summer of 1969, it dipped *below* the March 1966 level and continued downward. This was, then, another extended period of horizontal movement in stock prices.

THE INSTITUTIONAL SPECULATOR*

Investment based on genuine long-term expectations is so difficult today as to be scarcely practicable. He who attempts it must surely lead much more laborious days and run greater risks than he who tries to guess better than the crowd how the crowd will behave; and, given average intelligence, he may make more disastrous mistakes. Moreover, life is not long enough; human nature desires quick results, there is a peculiar zest in making money quickly, and remoter gains are discounted by the average man at a very high rate.

Although an extraordinarily accurate description of the present temper of the marketplace, these words of John Maynard Keynes are more than 30 years old. Let us see what meaning they have for us today.

The important question to consider is the degree to which current market trends are part of a dangerous speculative bubble or rather a sign of an important change in the character of security selection and investment. High levels of activity, in and of themselves, need not signify speculation.

---

* A Bernstein-Macaulay bulletin, May 1, 1966.

The Feel of the Market

The following table, based on data for March 1966, shows how much greater trading activity is running among a group of typical popular but better-class favorites than among the big blue chips:

	Shares Outstanding (millions)	Market Value ($ billions)	Trading in March (millions)	
			Shares	Dollars
American Telephone	529	30.2	2.2	128
General Motors	286	26.6	1.3	125
Standard Oil of New Jersey	215	16.6	0.6	46
General Electric	91	10.0	0.5	52
Du Pont	46	9.4	0.1	30
Sears, Roebuck	153	8.8	0.5	28
Union Carbide	60	3.9	0.5	32
American Electric Power	45	1.7	0.3	10
Total	1,425	107.2	6.0	451
Xerox	21	5.5	0.4	115
Polaroid	16	2.4	1.3	190
Boeing	8	1.4	1.0	166
Texas Instruments	5	1.2	0.3	76
Pan American Airways	15	1.1	1.8	134
Magnavox	7	1.0	1.3	156
Eastern Airlines	4	0.5	1.2	145
Fairchild Camera	3	0.5	1.4	258
Total	79	13.6	8.7	1,240

The contrasts are indeed dramatic:

- The total market value of the blue chips is about eight times as large as the total market value of the popular favorites, but the dollar volume of trading activity among the popular favorites was almost three times larger than in the blue chips.

- Only about one out of every 250 shares of the blue chips changed hands during March, but one out of every *nine* shares of the smaller companies changed hands. At the extremes, one out of every two shares of Fairchild Camera was traded as compared with only one out of every 420 shares in the case of General Motors. The pets of every bull market are always unusually active, but the activity in stocks like Fairchild Camera and Magnavox is worthy of notice by any standard.

- Although the table suggests it, the sheer magnitude of the big companies is almost beyond comprehension. For example, the total market value of American Telephone is larger than the total market value of all stocks listed on the American Stock Exchange. Indeed, just the *shrinkage* in market value of American Telephone and General Motors over the past 12 months is greater than the *total* market value of the eight popular favorites in our sample.

The source and significance of all this activity among the smaller companies is surely puzzling. The key to the puzzle, however, may lie precisely in this set of contrasts with the big blue chips.

The decline in the prices of the blue chips, as we all know, has been substantial and persistent: None of the eight major corporations in our sample has made a new all-time high for at least 11 months, and the group as a whole stands an average of 20 percent below those highs.

Meanwhile, however, even a small amount of money that normally went into the blue chips can have a tremendous effect when transferred to the smaller companies now in vogue. Five percent of the market value of the eight blue chips in our sample is equal to more than one-third of the total market value of the popular favorites. Indeed, just 5 percent of the total assets of the mutual funds would be enough to buy up more than 10 percent of the total market value of the eight favorites and more than the individual market values of all but the top two. If, as we suspect, money has been moving away from the blue chips in our sample, where earnings in 1965 were an average of 11 percent above 1964, and toward the popular favorites, where 1965 earnings were up 50 percent over 1964, the explosive character of both price and volume among the smaller companies should come as no surprise.

These trends are, of course, significant for all investors, but their greatest influence is on the behavior of the performance-conscious mutual funds. Institutional holdings of the eight blue chips in our sample are worth several times as much as their holdings of the eight popular favorites. Hence, even modest weakness among the blue chips can threaten the performance record of the funds unless spectacular results can be achieved elsewhere in the portfolio.

This is where we find the motivation for the extraordinary volume of activity in the stocks of the smaller companies. The gentle but apparently unremitting downward trend in the prices of the blue chips has been dragging down the value of institutional portfolios—as a result of which, institutional investment managers have allowed themselves to seek "instant performance" in the other sectors of the portfolio in an effort to achieve a record that their beneficiaries and stockholders will approve. Another important and significant consequence of these attitudes has been the total disregard of other companies, like the utilities and food stocks, where growth rates are strong and stable but still less sensational than among the leaders: The "laborious days" implied in the accumulation of stocks for the long pull require too much patience when the largest holdings in the portfolios are drifting downward.

Of course, all investors must devote some part of their available funds to seeking out dynamic new areas to replace those holdings whose performance may be below par. But the hectic character of the fad for "instant performance" is beating itself into cutthroat competition for tomorrow's big move and, like other fads, will ultimately lose its novelty and effectiveness as an investment policy.

Moreover, it is leading the institutions into gobbling up uncomfortably massive chunks of the outstanding shares of these companies, which means that they may literally run out of things to buy (in which case they may have to go back to the blue chips) or, if present trends continue uninterruptedly, that they will be willing to buy up companies of lower and lower quality and marketability.

Thus, the institutions run the risk of becoming the victims of their own emphasis on short-term performance and are indeed beginning to substitute speculation for investment. In so doing, they can lead all investors across the threshold of danger.

IS INSTITUTIONAL TRADING ACTIVITY EXCESSIVE?*

The impact of institutional trading on the security markets has recently excited so much discussion and argument among government regulators, financial operators, and academic agitators that we thought a little cool perspective on the subject might be useful to all concerned. While no question exists that institutions in general and mutual funds in particular are having an influence on the stock market, what we want to know is whether it is significantly different from the impact of individual investors and whether it is in any case baneful or salutory.

_____

* A Bernstein-Macaulay bulletin, September 1, 1967.

The best place to begin is with some sense of the orders of magnitude. In particular, there is no truth to the widely held impression that the mutual funds, pension funds, and insurance companies are gobbling up stock so fast that they will soon control American industry. Institutional stock ownership increased from 19 percent of all New York Stock Exchange listed companies in 1961 to 21 percent in 1966— hardly a dramatic change. Indeed, aside from the open-end mutual funds and the corporate pension funds (whose combined share rose from 9.2 percent to 11.4 percent), institutional share ownership is just about holding its own with individual share ownership.

One can also find exaggeration in the criticism of the abnormally high rate of turnover that is supposed to characterize institutional trading activity. The institutions referred to above, who hold about 21 percent of companies listed on the New York Stock Exchange, also account for less than 25 percent of total Exchange share volume: In other words, their average rate of portfolio turnover is little higher than that of individuals at the present time. And even this average is deceptive, for although the mutual funds have increased the turnover rate of their portfolios from a longtime annual average of around 20 percent to a level currently of nearly 40 percent, pension plans, insurance companies, foundations, and universities turn over their portfolios far less frequently (although they, too, are catching the fever of higher turnover).

Of course, it is popular at the present time to criticize the mutual funds for the frequency with which they make changes in their investments. They are usually accused either of churning portfolios to reward brokers for favors received or of a ruthless and heedless search for instant performance. Anyone who flatly denies these suggestions would be naïve, but if the mutual funds are vulnerable to criticism for too much activity, perhaps the less active portfolio managers may be equally vulnerable to criticism for too little.

We say this because we believe that many people ignore the vital and fundamental factors at work in the security markets that make greater turnover an inevitable rather than a strictly self-serving phenomenon.

In the first place, an increasingly aware and sophisticated investing public is behaving toward the mutual funds just as Adam Smith's Economic Man is supposed to behave: Investors are rewarding superior portfolio management by buying more of their shares and penalizing managers with subpar performance by redeeming more shares than they buy. This pattern has received less attention than it deserves, for it is surely a significant development. A mutual fund can no longer grow simply because it is located in Boston or has a Tiffany name or is managed by a leading investment banking house or has a large sales force. These characteristics were sufficient to attract investment money during the 1950s, but portfolio managers today are increasingly exposed to the harsh and impersonal discipline of the marketplace: An excess of redemptions over new sales is the inevitable consequence of inadequate performance. Surely no one who approves of the rewards and penalties of a free-enterprise system can disapprove of a trend that makes everyone try his best instead of resting on his laurels. And, in fact, increased competition among investment advisors for the management of pension-fund and other institutional portfolios may make life more difficult for their managers but is likely at the same time to improve their investment performance.

A second factor is also at work, even more fundamental in character: The old buy-and-hold investment philosophy no longer works and was in fact buried in the avalanche of 1962. Prior to that time, the same big blue chips and utility stocks always led the upturns that followed the large market breaks of 1937, 1946, and 1957, while the stocks of younger and more speculative enterprises lagged far behind. Any good security analyst could, without ever moving from his desk, predict with reasonable accuracy the future of the companies making up the backbone of his portfolios—the utilities, American Telephone, General Motors, General Electric, Jersey, Steel, and Sears. Thus, a respectable job of portfolio management was relatively easy and benefited the conservative over the aggressive investor. As the experience of the portfolios under our own management during this period amply illustrates, the fewer the changes made, the better the portfolios looked.

But the slow economic growth and profit squeeze of the late 1950s changed all this. Investors should now

28

realize that the big blue chips may be effective vehicles with which to play the cyclical swings in the economy, but those people who have continued from habit and inertia to cling indefinitely to their big winners of earlier decades have been destined to see their holdings fall behind more aggressively and imaginatively managed portfolios.

In our technologically oriented economy, portfolio management now requires more than college economics and a careful reading of the *Wall Street Journal*. Furthermore, on the frontier of growth, change is rapid. The security analyst must be alert, informed, and willing to abandon old favorites for new ones. Thus, we are wrong to accuse investment managers of being fickle when in truth nothing in a dynamic economy ever stands still.

Because of these influences, growing institutional share ownership may cause wider rather than narrower price changes in the future. Nevertheless, the momentum of these trends appears too strong for any pattern of regulation to blunt them to any significant degree.

What Happened Afterward:

Although the portion of institutional ownership of shares listed on the New York Stock Exchange increased from 1966 to 1968 by only about one percentage point, institutions became increasingly active traders over this period. Total purchases and sales of common stocks by noninsured, private pension funds, open-end investment companies, life-insurance companies, and fire and casualty companies amounted to $65 billion in 1968, just about double the level in 1966—and more than tenfold the volume of trading in 1958.

THE ANATOMY OF THE BEAR*

One of the few nice things about bear markets is that they are short-lived: The market goes down a lot faster than it goes up. If history is any guide, therefore, the present decline may well be close to touching bottom. This tells us little about how much farther it might go in the meantime or how many months must pass before we regain the old highs, but it does tell us that, if past patterns persist, we have at most only two or three more months of agony.

Excluding the extraordinary period of the 1930s, but going all the way back to 1916, we find that no major stock-market decline took more than 14 months to go from top to bottom,[†] no more than two (1916 and 1919) lasted more than nine months, and the average for all of them is only slightly over seven months. Indeed, an examination of a long-term chart of stock prices shows a large preponderance of rising months; over the past 50 years,

_____

* A Bernstein-Macaulay bulletin, August 1, 1966.

[†] The 1946 bear market had a secondary bottom that occurred a long time after completion of the first leg. This secondary bottom was so close to the original bottom, however, as to leave the essential point intact.

stock prices have been rising about two-thirds of the time—and this figure is increased to nearly three-quarters of the time if we exclude the Great Crash.

Another pleasant aspect of bear markets is that the early months are the worst, so that you get most of the damage over with in a hurry. Only in the cases of the 1916 and 1960 declines did the market fall off more sharply toward the end. The 10 percent drop in the summer of 1965 covered the whole distance in about two months, while all six postwar bear markets (1946, 1953, 1957, 1960, 1962, and 1965) recorded an average of 80 percent of the total drop in the first six months—and more than 90 percent if we exclude 1960.

None of this should be taken to suggest that bear markets are easy to live through, for prices fall much more steeply than they rise. Since World War II, stock prices have climbed at a monthly rate of about 1.5 percent during bull markets, but they have fallen at a monthly rate of about 5 percent during bear markets. Furthermore, postwar bear markets have been milder than their predecessors.

We can see this from another standpoint. The 1962 bear market lasted only six months from top to bottom, but at the bottom prices were back to where they had been a long 45 months before. Similarly, the 1957 decline lasted only three months, but in those three months the market lost as much as it gained in the entire preceding 30 months. And in 1932, prices were actually lower than they had been at any time since the outbreak of World War I. On the average, bear markets knock off in one month what bull markets require about four months to gain.

Why do these patterns repeat themselves so consistently? We believe the answer lies in the fundamental differences in the forces motivating buyers and sellers.

Over a long period of time, potential buying power will tend to outweigh selling pressures. One obvious reason, of course, is that stock prices should be expected to accompany the long-term upward trend in most economic indicators. Furthermore, savers are continuously accumulating cash for investment or transferring funds to financial intermediaries and fiduciaries that invest this money for them; financial managers are unlikely to hold it in short-term assets indefinitely. Perhaps equally important, but more difficult to prove, we all share an innate reluctance to sell stocks, particularly those which have treated us well over the years: We are willing to ride with them over brief periods of difficulty for fear of losing our position and missing out on the long-term uptrends.

Of course, for limited periods of time, the sellers do hold sway. Buyers withdraw or drop their bids and prices cascade downward. But while all the fundamental forces in our economy continuously replenish the sources of funds that can go back into the market, waves of selling seem to exhaust themselves relatively quickly. Most investors are not net sellers at all or will sell only a minor fraction of their holdings. The most astute will do it early before prices decline, but, having completed their selling, are now really potential buyers and have no more bearish impact.

As bad news spreads, the frightened dump their stocks, but the buyers are people who are acquiring stocks in the face of the bad news. Soon everyone who wants to sell has sold; those holding stocks have done so in full realization of whatever the bad news is about; bad news ceases to be a surprise that brings out new selling. The market, in short, is sold out and impervious to further unfavorable economic developments. Months may have to pass before the buyers take courage and come back—the 1946 high was not surpassed for five years and the 1937 high, for eight—but the downward movement has ended.

We currently see little that is likely to make stock prices rise significantly in the near future. The political uncertainties are, of course, important, and they in turn impinge upon the more fundamental influences of high interest rates and tight money. No major postwar upswing has begun without a prior change in monetary policy from tightness to ease.

On the other hand, the present situation has many of the earmarks of the dying days of previous bear markets. The Dow Jones Industrial Average made its high in February, just six months ago. Many top blue-chip stocks have been in a declining pattern for much longer than that. Everyone is looking at the same bad news and talking about it—the war, the money situation, gold and sterling, the riptides of social unrest. Further deterioration in these areas would come as no surprise. Hence, as most people anticipate them, most people probably have their portfolios in shape to face them.

But the future is always so full of surprises that some of those surprises could be good news: A settlement in Vietnam, an easing in the economy that would permit monetary policy to relax, a turn in the British situation are all possibilities. Then stock prices would revive and go back up again.

Meanwhile, however, even though the timing of the upturn is most uncertain, history suggests that the worst may be over and that it is too late to engage in a major program of liquidating common stocks.

What Happened Afterward:

At the beginning of August 1966, the Standard & Poor's industrial-stock average was under 90; it touched bottom in the month of October, when it reached 78; it rose above the August level by January 1967. Thus, anyone who sold in August stood a good chance of being whipsawed— he would have had to be very nimble to buy back much stock at prices below the levels at which he had done his selling, particularly after allowing for taxes and brokerage.

The main reason for the recovery in stock prices was suggested in the next to the last paragraph: Tight money had bitten so hard into the business expansion that the monetary authorities took the pressure off during the course of the last three months of the year; business activity flattened out and interest rates declined.

WHAT IS VOLUME TELLING US?*

The use of stock-exchange volume as a means of predicting the trend of stock prices rests upon a simple set of three facts and principles. Here they are in brief:

1. Volume tends to be higher when prices are rising than when they are falling.
2. Exceptions to this rule are both rare and short-lived. In most instances, particularly when prices decline on high volume, they indicate that a turn in stock prices is approaching.
3. Stock-market volume relative to the number of shares listed has held most of the time within a well-defined range, thereby enabling us to determine whether activity is normal or above or below normal.

Since prices and volume tend to move in the same direction, it follows that we can forecast the trend of the market if we can predict volume. We predict volume by determining whether activity is normal or abnormal; if it is abnormally high or low, it will, by definition, soon

---

* A Bernstein-Macaulay bulletin, April 1, 1967.

return to normal, and this change in direction is likely to be accompanied by a change in the direction of stock prices as well. This shift will occur sooner when volume is unsustainably low than when it is excessively high.

A careful analysis of the history of the stock market over the past 20 years shows that abnormally high volume preceded every major downturn with the exception of 1957 and that abnormally low volume preceded every major upturn. Indeed, *all* periods of abnormally low volume were followed by higher prices. Abnormally high volume, on the other hand, did give an occasional false signal, but, as we shall see shortly, with a sufficient degree of consistency to lend more rather than less reliability to the forecasting procedure.

What would we consider normal volume today? History tells us that, over the past 20 years, the number of shares traded on the New York Stock Exchange each year has never fallen below 12 percent of the number of shares listed and has exceeded 19 percent only once (1950). Since 1957, annual turnover has fallen below 14 percent in only three years—1957, 1960, and 1962, all of which were clear bear-market years. (We calculate the annual turnover rate at any time by multiplying the daily level of activity by 250, the approximate number of trading days in each year, and then dividing by the number of shares listed.)

If activity falls much below an annual rate of 15 percent turnover for a month or so, this would be an unsustainably low level; volume is therefore likely to rise; if volume rises, so will prices. On the other hand, if turnover exceeds 20 percent or more for a period of months, we can expect volume and prices to turn downward.

The 1965–1966 period provides an excellent illustration of this. In July and August 1965, following the May–June market decline, turnover ran at only 12 percent—a distinctly bullish pattern. The market turned upward in September, accompanied by 19 to 20 percent turnover through November. But volume continued to mount with prices right through to April 1966, when the Dow Jones Industrials were already past their peak but when many individual stocks and more representative averages made their record highs. Volume in these months averaged nearly nine million shares a day, almost double the level of July and August 1965, and equal to 21 to 23 percent annual rates of turnover. This was a decisive bearish signal.

The market dipped in May, followed by the major part of the crash in the June–September period. Turnover in June and July was about normal for a declining market—14 percent. It then rose to 17 percent in August in the face of sharply falling prices, suggesting the possibility of an approaching turn. In September it sank to an abnormally low level of 13 percent, a daily average of only 5.7 million shares. This was further confirmation of an upswing in the near future.

As these patterns predicted, every month since September has seen prices on an upbeat, accompanied by steadily rising volume as well. Volume has risen so far, in fact, that the danger signals are flying again: Since early

January, activity has run consistently above nine million shares a day, which, with about 11 billion shares listed, means turnover is back up over the 20 percent level.

As activity at this level for an entire year would seem most unlikely on the basis of past experience, volume at some point in the near future is going to subside, which in turn suggests lower prices as well.

While this is clearly cause for caution, we see three other considerations indicating that any decline in prices is likely to be either mild or some distance off in time:

1. Turnover has been running over 20 percent for only three months, a relatively short period of time. It exceeded this level for almost six months before the 1966 break and for eight months during 1961.

2. As institutional investors in general and mutual funds in particular become more performance-minded and account for a larger portion of stock ownership, we may have to step up our definition of "normal." This is particularly the case in view of the type of churning in which the funds engage during bull markets.

3. We have already mentioned that abnormally high volume has occasionally given us a false signal of an approaching downturn. Each of these false signals, however, has come *early* in a major upswing. December 1949–January 1950 and November 1954–March 1955 are clear examples of this phenomenon and were excellent times for the purchase of common

stocks. Thus, abnormally high volume early in an upswing may be a confirmation of vigor rather than of its approaching demise.

What this means, in short, is that continuation of annual turnover rates in excess of 20 percent—say, more than nine million shares a day—for another two or three months would justify a program of pruning common-stock positions, but that, at this moment, no major shift to a more conservative investment policy is justified by the volume signals.

Of course, in Washington and elsewhere, recognition is spreading that we have passed through a major business-cycle peak, as our January 1 bulletin predicted. On balance, however, we believe that the indications for the stock market are constructive: the long duration of the 1966 decline (see our bulletin of August 1, 1966), the tendency of the stock market to anticipate rather than to accompany lower earnings, and the natural move toward easier money during recessions are all major considerations in investment policy. Taken together with the volume patterns described above, we believe that the downside risks continue to be limited.

What Happened Afterward:

Stock prices continued upward for six months after the publication of this bulletin and then flattened out. There was a brief and shallow dip during the first quarter of 1968, after which prices again took off for nine months more. Hence, the "constructive" indications mentioned in this bulletin were valid; the "downside risks" were clearly "limited."

THE NEW DIMENSIONS OF TRADING ACTIVITY*

The terrible clerical jam that has overtaken the back offices of Wall Street firms has a significance that extends far beyond the frustrations and short tempers that have followed in its wake. History tells us that stock prices correlate closely with trading activity, bull markets being associated with high volume and bear markets with low. Thus, the really interesting question is whether we are going to remain on this plateau of unexpectedly high volume—or will activity and stock prices sink lower?

In the spring of 1959, Bernstein-Macaulay was retained by the New York Stock Exchange to prepare projections of trading activity on the Exchange for 1970 and 1980. At that time, a more or less mechanical projection of trends that had characterized the preceding 13 years or so indicated average daily volume on the order of six million shares for the late 1960s—just about one-half of the level we are currently witnessing. This is dramatic evidence of how the parameters have since shifted to an entirely different order of magnitude, particularly when we recall that some of the powers that be at the Exchange in 1959 were extremely

---

* A Bernstein-Macaulay bulletin, July 1, 1968.

dubious about even our six-million-share figure (which was about double average daily volume in 1958–1959).

While this was our "normal" projection, we also provided for the possibility of a "boom-and-bust" type market. Thus, the normal projection had provided for annual share volume equal to 10 to 15 percent of the number of shares listed, but the boom-and-bust projection set its high turnover rates in the 19 to 24 percent range. As these turnover rates had in fact been reached in 1943, 1945, 1946, 1950, 1954, 1955, and the last six months of 1958, they were by no means unreasonable in the light of experience.

Actual events have confirmed the accuracy of our forecasts. From 1960 to 1965, annual turnover was in line with the normal projection, varying between 12 percent and 15 percent of the shares listed. But then turnover moved up to 18 percent in 1966 and hit 22 percent in 1967; so far this year, it has been running at an annual rate of 25 percent, with a few weeks of 29 to 30 percent. Thus, current activity levels were in fact provided for in our 1959 analysis, although we doubt whether anyone, including ourselves, took them very seriously in an environment in which "Buy the blue chips and hold them" was the hallmark of performance.

Is the present rate of turnover sustainable? This is the crucial question. A return to more normal levels of activity would imply a bear market of serious dimensions. Both the 1962 and the 1966 bear markets were preceded by turnovers in the 25 percent area followed by a drop to the 10 to 13 percent area as the market declined. During the recent baby bear market of September 1967 to March 1968, incidentally, the low point in volume was still rather high—an annual turnover rate of about 17 percent, but it had run above 25 percent during only one week in August and one week in September.

The major change in the parameters has been the almost incredibly sharp surge in trading activity on the part of institutional investors, even as their proportion of total common shares outstanding has been rising. This has been particularly the case with the mutual funds, but the rapid growth in both size and activity of noninsured pension funds has also had a significant impact.

From 1956 to 1965, annual purchases and sales of common stock by mutual funds varied little from a level equal to about 20 percent of their total holdings. In 1966, this ratio moved to 33 percent; it hit 41 percent in 1967. At the same time, their holdings of common stocks listed on the Exchange rose from less than 4 percent of the total in 1956 to about 5.5 percent currently. Pension-fund activity in common stocks was equal each year to about 10 percent of their holdings during the 1956–1965 period, with the trend in their turnover rate actually declining; last year it was up to almost 20 percent. Over this same period, their holdings of listed stocks increased from about 3 percent of the total to more than 7 percent.

Data published by the Exchange indicate that mutual funds and pension funds together accounted for more than one-third of all purchases and sales on the New York Stock

Exchange in 1967, compared with less than one-fifth in 1959. Indeed, it appears that these two groups of institutions accounted for almost half of the increase in total share volume between 1965 and 1967.

Hence, major institutional investors have at least doubled their turnover rates, while turnover in the market as a whole has gone up about 50 percent. Seen from this viewpoint, the sharp rise in annual turnover rates on the New York Stock Exchange must be associated in large part with increased institutional buying and selling. Other investors would seem to have become only somewhat more active on the New York Stock Exchange than they were previously—or are concentrating much more of their trading on the American Exchange and over-the-counter, where turnover rates are far in excess of anything seen at any point in recent or relevant experience.

We think these facts are extremely significant. During activity peaks in the past that were followed by bear markets, public trading accelerated as rapidly as or more rapidly than institutional trading; by its very nature, it was likely to be unsustainable. On the other hand, the current intense drive for performance by precisely those share owners who enjoy a continuous net inflow of funds—the mutuals, the pension funds, the insurance companies, the educational institutions, and the bank trust departments—is likely to lead to levels of stock trading that will continue to look high relative to past history. Since entire weeks running two to three times the daily average and entire months up to double the daily average have been seen frequently in the past, 20-million-share days should really cause little surprise; with about 12 billion shares listed, activity of less than 10 million shares a day should be much more of a surprise.

Thus, while our experience with these new patterns is still too brief for us to make any hard predictions based on recent trends in share volume, the analysis does suggest that (barring a major change in regulative procedures) what seems like feverish activity, on the New York Stock Exchange at least, is probably much less ominous today than it would have been under different structural conditions.

What Happened Afterward:

There was one 20-million-share day during the month that followed the publication of this bulletin and two more in October 1968, neither of which was followed by any significant decline in stock prices. Activity for the year as a whole averaged 13 million shares a day, with no month after July (and on into the first half of 1969) averaging less than 10 million shares daily.

THE GOLD CRISIS AND
THE SECURITY MARKETS*

The investor who attempts to frame his strategy in times such as these has a hard time of it indeed. Money and gold

---

* A Bernstein-Macaulay bulletin, April 1, 1968.

themselves are abstract, confusing, complex, even terrifying. Newspaper articles, television commentators, soothing statesmen's statements, vaguely remembered lessons from college economics, and the usual rumor mills of Wall Street assault our brain and intensify rather than relieve our sense of uneasiness and fear. No one really tells us what will happen or what to do if whatever it is does happen.

This bulletin will therefore—as briefly as possible—attempt to answer three questions:

1. What happened?
2. What is likely to happen now?
3. What is the investment climate going to be?

During the first 10 years or so after World War II by choice, and since the passing of the Suez crisis of 1956–1957 by apparent necessity, the United States has been spending abroad more than foreigners have been spending here. This has both depleted our gold stock and increased the number of dollars held by foreigners.

Yet, most of the time, the dollar seemed to be a very strong currency. Our economic power remained unchallenged. Inflation here was less severe than in Western Europe or Japan. Our exports comfortably exceeded our imports. We accumulated an enormous array of highly profitable investments in foreign countries whose total output adds up to the third major world economic power. Our well-balanced economic growth and prosperity were the envy of the world.

45

All this was true until the President decided in late 1965 to escalate the war in Vietnam. Then three unpleasant effects of this step hit the dollar hard:

1. Our military outlays abroad turned sharply higher (and a lot of the money spent in Vietnam ends up in French banks).
2. The overheating of the domestic economy sparked a significant increase in imports from other countries.
3. The war itself created among Europeans a crisis of confidence in American leadership and in our uses of power, leading in turn to a desire to humiliate or at least to humble us.

Pressures, doubts, and controversy swirled through the world's financial centers as the President refused to recommend Spartan measures to avoid a financial crisis in 1966 and then the Congress refused to act on his belated suggestions in 1967. As disturbed foreign governments and central banks cashed in their dollars for gold, foreign private individuals also adopted the traditional signal of distrust and turned their money into gold. Making no effort whatsoever to introduce any element of risk into this situation, the United States poured its golden treasure into the hands of the speculators in an effort to hold the price of gold down to $35 an ounce. And the more the gold reserves were depleted, the greater the chance that the price of gold would have to go up someday—and the more intense the speculation.

The British devaluation last November made an ultimate crisis impossible to avoid. First of all, it proved that even Anglo-Saxon statesmen are capable of gigantic and tragic untruths—whether it be "We shall never devalue" or "We seek no wider war." Second, it showed that large-scale speculation can be self-justifying in its momentum, quite independent of the underlying fundamentals of the situation.

Through all of this, the speculators took no risk. Most forms of speculation do involve risks, so that the speculator performs a useful economic function in assuming those risks. But when you can sell sterling at $2.80 and be sure that you can always repurchase at no more than $2.80, and when you can buy gold at $35 and always be sure you can resell at no less than $35, why not take a chance? The wonder is that the crisis took so long to develop.

The closing of the London gold pool now means that speculators in gold will have to pay more than $35 an ounce. While perhaps they will end up with a profit, they are also exposed for the first time to the possibility that they may have to take a loss. This is the most important consequence of this excessively delayed and highly welcome decision.

At the same time, however, the United States has been forced to promise to deflate its not altogether overheated economy. Higher taxes, reduced government spending, and higher interest rates are the order of the day. As we pointed out last month, these steps are unlikely to reduce prices. They will, however, reduce incomes and employment and hence should lead to a decline in our imports from abroad. *The unemployed, in short, will make the major contribution to the preservation of our gold stock. Those who watch them riot this summer will do well to keep this aspect of sound finance in mind.* We can only hope that the Europeans live up to their side of the bargain and deflate through lower interest rates and a willingness to import more from us.

We are about to witness the remarkable spectacle of an administration pursuing in an election year an unpopular war and deflationary economic policies to boot. It remains to be seen whether these programs can survive the social strains and stresses they incur. As the *New York Times* argued in a recent editorial,

> It would be a serious mistake to save the [international monetary] system if the cost is widespread unemployment, a marked retreat in the war on poverty, and an abandonment of attempts to rebuild the cities and root out the ghettos.

The contradictions here are obvious, and, as they say in the song, something's got to give.

Social pressures are not going to give way, of that we may be sure. Happily, perhaps, the war will come to an end or at least deescalate. If it does not, the international monetary system may well go down the drain because it will be unable to contain the pressures from the other forces.

If that happens, let us remember that Americans will still do business with one another in dollars and that a dollar will buy neither less nor more at home than it would buy anyway. Foreign investment and foreign trade may be severely hampered, which will be serious for some sectors of our economy but surely not for all. It will, however, have more serious consequences for our friends abroad, which explains their eagerness to keep the structure viable and which may in the end save us from some kind of a complete disaster and breakdown.

Despite this less than optimistic appraisal of the situation, we believe that investors should be prepared to take a more hopeful view toward the security markets in the very near future. This unorthodox opinion is based on the following considerations.

First, the war is obviously going to end someday. When it does, all of the parameters are going to shift, rapidly and radically. The direct and indirect impact on many industries will be tremendous. The investor who waits for this magic moment to arrive will face the genuine possibility that he will be buying in too late in the game.

Second, as our bulletin of August 1966 demonstrated in detail, bear markets tend to be much shorter in time than bull markets, and this particular bear market—remarkably mild as it has been—is showing signs of age. It is already deep into its sixth month. Postwar history indicates that

75 to 80 percent of the total damage of a bear market is done during the first six months and that major oversold conditions develop within eight to nine months. Unless something very unusual is afoot at the present time, therefore, we should touch or pass the bottom somewhere within the next six to eight weeks.

Third, gloom, pessimism, fear, skepticism, even revulsion are thick in the financial markets today. Bad news is widely anticipated and expected. Most portfolios are adjusted to absorb the worst. Billions in cash are awaiting the moment for the tide to turn. No unpleasant news will catch anyone by surprise. On the other hand, good news could cause a stampede, just because of the element of surprise.

Finally, the more serious turn of fiscal policy is likely to lead to lower long-term interest rates. Although some of the pressures on the balance-of-payments problem will perhaps move short-term interest rates higher, the result on the corporate bond market will probably be bullish. As our readers know, we believe that the stock market is strongly influenced by interest rates and will always behave well in periods of rising bond prices and falling interest rates.

There is, in short, much to be hopeful about. The tangible evidence of international monetary cooperation is fully apparent. Political forces are pushing for peace. The deflationary imperatives of the gold crisis are bullish for bonds and therefore for stocks. Bad news is so generously shared among investors that it can hardly damage security prices very much from here on out.

What Happened Afterward:

As this bulletin was written, the leading stock-market averages were within one or two percentages of their lows for the month of March. On the first day of trading in April, right after President Johnson's historic television address on Sunday night, March 31, 1968, the market closed 2.5 percent above the March 29 closing. Prices rose about 9 percent for the month of April as a whole and climbed a total of 20 percent or so between the time this bulletin was written and when prices topped out just eight months later. There was, in short, "much to be hopeful about."

GROWTH COMPANIES VERSUS GROWTH STOCKS*

Growth companies have received so much attention in recent years that the term threatens to become our leading economic cliché. Whether it is management leadership, national importance, or simply prudent investment that one seeks to find, the method is always the same: look to the growth company.

---

* From the *Harvard Business Review*, Vol. 34, No. 5, September–October 1956. Copyright © 1956 by the President and Fellows of Harvard College; all rights reserved.

But what is a growth company? Is it a company characterized by unusual technological activity and innovation? Is it merely a company whose sales and earnings have risen more rapidly than most? And what is a growth stock? Are all securities of "growth companies" *ipso facto* growth stocks?

The questions are deceptively simple—but tremendously important. If the phrase "growth company" is to blanket every company that does research or is doing more business this year than it did five or ten years ago, the term will be so broad as to be utterly useless. Only if we can pin it down to a practical, workable definition can we hope to distinguish it in a useful way from the concept of "growth stock."

The object of this article is not only to try to provide answers to these questions but also to demonstrate two rather heretical—but, I believe, constructive—points of view: (1) that growth companies constitute a very small and select rather than a broad and important roster of corporate enterprises; and (2) that growth stocks are a happy or haphazard category of investments which, curiously enough, have little or nothing to do with growth companies.

It should be emphasized, however, that stocks of some companies that do not meet the criteria of growth used here may appreciate in value just as much as stocks of companies that do, and the stocks of some companies that do fulfill the criteria may turn out to do less well. There are many accidental factors that can influence the results, not the least of which is concerted misjudgment by investors. But the point is that, by and large and over a period of time, the factors of true growth, being more fundamental, are more likely to be a reliable guide for the future than are past increases in market price or current evaluation by the market—or, at least, than either of these without the addition of the particular growth concept set forth here.

Later in this article I shall outline a new statistical method of analysis that demonstrates the soundness of this proposition and implements it for action.

Economic development or growth occurs in three different processes: in the increase of population, in the accumulation of capital, and in the technological progress that enables us to produce more things, better things, different things, or the same things more cheaply.

Each of these growth processes affects a business differently. As a businessman, the individual executive or owner can have no direct influence on the first of these three factors; his business may be affected *by* it, but he cannot have any effect *on* it. Not so with the other possibilities for growth, however; these are internally generated by business firms on their own initiative. This point is basic to the whole matter: *True growth is organic and comes from within.*

A good way to pinpoint the distinguishing characteristics of a growth company is to look at five cases that show what a growth company is *not*. Bear in mind that the crucial question is whether the firm's expansion is the result of internally determined conditions or simply a response to external events over which it has no control.

1. A company that expands by acquiring other outfits is not a growth company. The acquisitions, once absorbed, may so change its character that it later becomes a growth company, but the process of expansion by acquisition *as such* is not growth in our terms here.

2. Firms whose business increases simply because they serve growing markets are not growth companies, for they are not causing the market to grow but are only responding passively to outside events. Of course, we must also resist being dazzled by an impressive earnings progression resulting largely from a company's ability to raise its prices in a sellers' market faster than its costs go up.

   For example, it is fashionable to consider the oil companies in the growth class. Certainly their sales and earnings have expanded impressively. However, the growth in their operations has resulted primarily from a rising demand for oil that the oil companies themselves have capitalized on but did very little to create. Without the rising automobile population, the high volume of construction (which created the demand for space heating) and the growth of other industries (like electric power) that use oil for fuel, there would have been very much less expansion in the oil industry.

3. Most of the paper companies should probably be excluded from the growth-company group, although they usually are included. The lines of demarcation are admittedly a little fuzzy here, for some of these companies have developed new products or found new uses for paper that did not exist in the past. Essentially, however, they have benefited from the burgeoning demand for paper for packaging, for newspapers and magazines, for paper towels, tissues, napkins, and so forth. This rising demand was a function of higher industrial production, higher incomes, and increased population; the paper companies took advantage of these developments but had little to do with causing them to come about.

4. Some observers have even gone so far as to call the steel industry a growth industry in recent years. It is true that the financial results of the big steel companies have been outstanding even when compared with the most successful growth companies, and it is also a fact that the per capita consumption of steel is rising persistently. However, with modest exceptions, the steel companies are still selling to the same old markets (73 percent of steel consumption in 1955 was accounted for by automobiles, construction, machinery, and containers), and it is the growth of those markets that explains the rising demand for steel.

To be sure, new uses for steel have been developed, but either they have been worked out *in response to* a need first expressed by the customers, as in the case of certain stainless steels, or they do not make a significant contribution to the earnings of the big producers. Furthermore, the steel industry's earnings are unusually dependent on the maintenance of a highly inflated price structure, which has gone up more than twice as fast as the average of all nonagricultural commodities since the period 1947–1949 (as compared, for instance, with only a nominal increase in the price of chemicals). If steel prices were pushed back to 1947–1949 levels, all the steel companies would operate at substantial losses. This would not be the case with most true growth companies.

5. As a general rule, it would seem that most raw-material producers have to be excluded from the growth-company category, partly because their growth is dependent on the demand for final products that they can have little influence on, and partly because substantial increases in earnings are basically the result of inflated prices. An obvious and significant exception to this statement is the aluminum industry. The demand for aluminum has grown and is growing phenomenally, not simply because the major consumers of aluminum are doing more business than they used to do but, perhaps more important, because the aluminum companies themselves have found so many new uses for the metal, and therefore so many new consumers of it. The aluminum industry is carving out its own market.

The Feel of the Market

The ability to create its own market is, in fact, the strategic, the dominating, and the single most distinguishing characteristic of a true growth company.

The reason for this is not simply that the development of new products, new processes, and new uses for old products leads to higher sales and bigger profits. More important is the fact that the *quality* of a growth company's sales and earnings is fundamentally different from that of other companies.

A new product or a highly differentiated one is, for a brief period of time at least, unique; it has a virtual monopoly. There is only one Terramycin, one Dacron, one Univac, one Centravac; but the identical steel can be bought from Bethlehem or United States Steel, and the same copper, from Kennecott or from Anaconda. Thus, growth-company products tend to provide larger-than-average profit margins and to postpone or possibly even eliminate the danger of price competition. At the same time, the continuous development of new products and new markets offsets declining sales in old products and, perhaps most important of all, tends to insulate the company from many of the hazards of general economic trends.

In short, the real growth company is, to borrow sociologist David Riesman's phrase, "inner-directed" rather than "other-directed." It is a nonconformist in economic society. It adapts the outside world to itself by creating something or a demand for something that did not exist before, instead of adapting itself to changes in the outside world. It does not necessarily grow faster than the economy as a whole, but it does grow faster than the markets in which its products are sold.

This is why so many (but by no means all) of the chemical, electrical-equipment, and electronic companies fall into the true growth-company class. These companies are at the dynamic and technological frontiers of our society and are continuously developing new uses for old products, new products to replace old products, new products with new functions, and new processes for turning out goods and services of all types.

But the creation of a market does not depend solely on the introduction of a new product or a new use for an old product. A market can be created in less glamorous industries, where dynamic merchandising creates such strong brand loyalty that consumers are convinced the product is unique and hence abandon other products in its favor. Growth, in other words, need not be the result of creating *new* demand; it can occur when a company wins a larger share of existing markets. For example:

Scott Paper Company has a fundamentally different character from most of the other paper companies and a far more successful earnings record. Of course, Scott Paper has developed new products or tangibly improved versions of old products, but in reality its merchandise is part of the stuff of everyday life. Yet Scott's merchandising methods to both the general public and to its important market among manufacturers and institutions have brought it unusually close to its customers and have created the feeling of assurance that its products *are* of superior quality.

As a result, Scott has more influence over its market than most other paper companies. Its success as an active rather than passive agent in the economy is dramatically illustrated by the way it persistently increased its earnings during the Great Depression and by the degree to which the growth in its earnings has markedly outpaced the rest of the industry in recent years.

Growth potentials can emerge where one least expects to find them, particularly where new markets are developed for old products. An intriguing development in this connection is the effort of the chewing-gum manufacturers to take advantage of the salesmanship of the American GI in developing a taste for chewing gum in foreign countries during the war.

Perhaps my point can best be brought out by asking whether the successful automobile companies are growth companies. A good case can be made for the argument that they do not meet the criteria. The automobile is no longer a new product. A major share of the cars sold today are replacements rather than first purchases of a car. The expansion in the automobile market has largely been the result of a rising population and a higher level of personal incomes, and in this sense the automobile companies have been adapting to outside conditions rather than creating their own market.

Yet, when one studies what has happened in this industry in recent years, one wonders whether there is not another side to the question. Through dramatic and persistent changes in style and engineering, the automobile companies *have* created a new product and made old ones obsolete. Who can say whether the $3,000 car of 1956 with all its new gadgets is or is not more expensive than the same $2,000 brand in 1946? If the creation of new products has not been achieved, how else can we explain the fabulous success of the 1955 models, introduced during a recession and when most statistical tests indicated that the automobile market was well saturated? Does not the effort to sell a second car to every family open up a potentially enormous market? Thus, at least the leading companies in the industry would seem to come close to qualifying as growth companies.

As I am sure most readers are aware, there are many definitions of a growth company, and I do not claim that the one just outlined is the "last word." But it is, to my mind, a useful concept for the specific purpose of distinguishing the selected group of really dynamic, pioneering firms from the general run of well-managed firms. In particular, it should aid us in refining, building upon, and carrying a step further Robert W. Anderson's provocative analysis in the March–April 1955 issue of *Harvard Business Review*, "Unrealized Potentials in Growth Stocks."

It will be remembered that Anderson would include as a growth company any firm that shows expansion, whether or not the impulse comes from within the organization itself. For example, in connection with his belief that growth companies are likely to turn up only in growth industries, he has this to say:

> Such an industry should be a basic element in the country's standard of living, and it should have existing products or services which have met with such increasing public acceptance that unit demand is rising at an average rate significantly greater than the average rate of unit growth of the economy as a whole, although not necessarily dramatic.

But within these terms—and this is the significant point—we could include the major elements of industries such as construction, food, fertilizer, and printing, where growth has been to a major extent a response to expanding demand rather than the creator of it, and where, furthermore, the financial results of the vast majority of companies have been mediocre, to say the least, and have been far from immune to the business cycle.

The remainder of Anderson's analysis establishes certain criteria, such as research programs, product and process planning, attitudes of management, and so on, which no growth company can be without. But are not these the characteristics that, by and large, one should seek in *any* well-managed company? Standard Oil of New Jersey, as a case in point, would probably meet Anderson's criteria every bit as well as, say, Scott Paper or Minnesota Mining and Manufacturing. However, if the emphasis is on the difference between active and passive growth, there can be no question that Scott and 3M are growth companies, while there would be a substantial measure of doubt about Standard Oil of New Jersey in that regard.

Now let us turn from the qualitative criteria of growth companies to the expression of those criteria in financial performance. A growth company's sales and earnings should be expected to show a rising trend, and the trend should climb more steeply than the average. "Results are what count."

For instance, the sheer size of appropriations for research and merchandising—sometimes used as a criterion—by itself means nothing. In fact, such expenses are "down the drain," since (1) they cannot justifiably be capitalized, (2) they cannot be turned off without running the risk that the company will lose its position, and (3) a large proportion of selling and research expense can only lay a foundation for future growth and does not bring in any immediate return. Activities of this sort can pay off only if they ultimately bring in substantial returns that will both recapture the money "down the drain" and provide a high return on capital; and the more expensive they are, the truer this is.

Actually, even a better-than-average uptrend in sales and earnings is not enough. A true growth company's financial results should meet the following four test criteria as well:

1. The uptrend in earnings should be relatively smooth. Earnings need not rise every single year, but they should increase in more years than they decrease, and they should show an increase in at least as many years as the "average" company's earnings increase.

2. What is true of earnings should also be true, in most cases, of dividends. There is little point in buying a stock yielding 2 percent or 3 percent unless over a reasonable period it pays out more than a fixed-income security or less "dynamic" stock.

3. Certainly, return on net worth should be maintained; and if the dividend payout is abnormally low, then return on net worth should actually be rising. In other words, the stockholder's money that is reinvested instead of paid out should earn at least as much as the old capital that produced these earnings. This ratio is indeed the most significant indicator of management's overall ability and aggressiveness.

4. Increases in earnings and/or net worth should, of course, reflect an increase in the physical volume of output or at least a beneficial shift in product mix—rather than merely larger dollar results reflecting a rising price level.

Now, financial performance has the added advantage of being readily subject to statistical measurement.

Let us take Anderson's list of 25 "growth companies" and add to that list eight additional companies and subject them to a series of financial tests to see how the quantitative and qualitative characteristics of growth companies mesh.

Here is the list of companies in the sample (those marked with an asterisk are the eight companies I have added to Anderson's list):

Amerada

American Can

American Cyanamid*

Bethlehem Steel*

Continental Oil

Corning Glass*

Dow Chemical

Du Pont

Eastman Kodak

General Electric

General Motors*

Hartford Fire Insurance

Hercules Powder

Humble Oil

IBM

Insurance Co. of
    North America

International Paper*

Johns-Manville

Libbey-Owens-Ford

Minneapolis Honeywell

Monsanto Chemical

National Lead*

National Steel

Owens Illinois

J. C. Penney

Scott Paper*

Sears, Roebuck

Standard Oil of California

Standard Oil of New Jersey

Union Carbide and Carbon

U.S. Steel*

U.S. Gypsum

Westinghouse Electric

This is by no means an all-inclusive list of growth companies. Conversely, quite a few of the companies in the sample are not growth companies at all, at least in terms of our qualitative criteria. But this very makeup should help to sharpen the distinction between our concept of growth companies and the usual idea of growth stocks.

Here are the tests to which I subjected the financial data on these companies:

For the 33 companies, I compared 1947–1949 average data with 1953–1955 average data. The two periods are sufficiently separated in time to be revealing. Also, each includes a recession year, a reasonably good year, and a boom year.

All data were converted to a per-share basis, adjusted for stock dividends and stock splits—that is, they were expressed in terms of the number of shares outstanding at the end of 1955.

For each company, I calculated the following:

Number of years of rising earnings;

Number of years of rising dividends;

Percentage increase in earnings, 1947–1949 to 1953–1955;

Percentage increase in dividends, 1947–1949 to 1953–1955;

Return on book value, 1947–1949 and 1953–1955;

Ratio of price to 1953–1955 average earnings, December 31, 1955;

Ratio of price to increase in average annual earnings from 1947–1949 to 1953–1955, December 31, 1955.

The data largely confirm the ability of companies that fulfill the qualitative criteria to meet the financial tests as well. For instance, the five companies whose earnings show the greatest percentage increase between 1947–1949 and 1953–1955 include four clear examples of true growth companies (marked with asterisks), all but one of which, Scott Paper, increased the return on net worth:

Corning Glass*	up 300%
National Lead*	up 174%
Du Pont*	up 109%
Scott Paper*	up 106%
U.S. Steel	up 103%

On the other hand, the five companies whose earnings show the least increase over the period include only one that seems to fulfill our qualitative criteria of a growth company (marked with asterisk):

Westinghouse Electric*	up 0%
Hartford Fire Insurance	up 3%
Continental Oil	up 4%
J. C. Penney	up 6%
Humble Oil	up 13%

The same correspondence between increased earnings and growth criteria shows up throughout the whole list, though not quite to the same degree. With special or temporary circumstances always in the picture to alter or mask the financial results, there are bound to be some companies that have the qualitative requirements of a growth company but fail to meet the financial test (at least for the short run), and at the same time some companies that do not fulfill the qualitative criteria but show superior financial results (although it is a good question whether this superiority would persist through all economic vicissitudes).

Accordingly, the items comprising our financial test do make an effective tool for screening out companies that fulfill the qualitative criteria we have established for true growth. If it works four times out of five, or anywhere near that much, that is a high rate of reliability, particularly when compared with the statistical basis of increased market value as used by Anderson. Indeed, the following five facts raise the fundamental question whether any list selected like Anderson's 25 companies is representative of growth situations in terms of either company or stock:

1. Only 10 of the 25 companies showed an increase in earnings over the 1947–1949 base that was better than the increase in earnings of the Dow Jones Industrial Average. (Although the 30 companies in the Dow Jones Industrial Average are used to represent the average company in this discussion, the Moody's industrial average of 125 companies would have resulted in only minor and insignificant differences in results.)

2. Only 13 of them raised their dividends by more than the increase in the dividend on the Dow Jones Industrial Average.

3. Only two increased the rate of return on book value between 1947–1949 and 1953–1955. As a matter of fact, only seven of the 33 companies in the analysis achieved this result. If we seek the number of companies that more or less maintained their rate of return, say, within two percentage points, then we can still add only five companies to this list.

4. The earnings on the Dow Jones Industrial Average rose in three out of the five years 1947–1952 and in six out of the eight years 1947–1955. But nine of the 25 companies failed to equal this result in the shorter period, and 14 of them failed to do so in the longer period.

5. The dividend on the Dow Jones Industrial Average was increased four times during 1947–1952 and seven times during 1947–1955. But 15 of the 25 companies increased their dividends less than four times in the shorter period (nine of them increased their dividends less than three times) and 20 failed to do as well as the Dow Jones Industrial Average in the longer period (11 failed to increase their dividends even five times).

The data are revealing in another sense. They suggest that *superior financial results are apparently not the fortuitous outcome of being a member of a growth industry.* Instead, such results seem to reflect significant differences in management concepts, policies, and techniques. Wide variations in performance appear among companies in the same industry; for example, compare General Electric with Westinghouse, Bethlehem with National Steel, Du Pont with Union Carbide or Monsanto, Standard Oil of New Jersey with Continental Oil. Again, General Motors has an outstanding statistical record, but perhaps only one of its competitors would show up as well as does the average of the 33 companies; and the same is substantially the case with IBM and its competitors.

This is not to say that the stocks of all the companies that our list singles out as leaders are necessarily good buys for the future or, on the other hand, that the stocks of all the others can be expected to perform poorly in the years ahead. For instance, Hercules Powder appears lackluster, but actually it may have a growth potential today that few of the companies in the list can match.

The point here is simply that any broad generalizations drawn from statistical comparisons can be misleading when it comes to the selection of individual stocks for future appreciation. Qualitative analysis must also be brought to bear—to explore for special circumstances and, in particular, to determine to what extent the company exhibits the characteristics we have been discussing: that is, whether it dynamically creates its own markets, has quasi-monopolistic features reflected in higher profit margins, is sufficiently inner-directed to be relatively immune to business fluctuations, and has turned in a consistent record of growth in earning power, dividends, and return on net worth.

Furthermore, one other dimension must be added—market price—before we have anything that can serve as a guide to investment opportunity. As a matter of fact, the statistical method itself must be more refined before it can be really useful for the purposes under consideration.

Hence, let us tackle the specific problem of what all this means to the investor who is looking for appreciation in value. The factors we have been discussing—particularly higher-than-average profit margins and superior growth in earning power, dividend payments, and return on net worth—obviously affect market values and are therefore of considerable interest to the investor. And, needless to say, the market effect is also of considerable importance to the growth company's management, for the investor's decisions influence the supply of equity capital. But do these factors dominate market value, or at least influence it to such an extent that growth companies are likely to be synonymous with growth stocks, and growth stocks with superior buys? That is the question.

One of the quickest and most forceful ways to answer this question is to turn again to Anderson's list of 25 corporations. This list, as we have already seen, includes a substantial group of companies that do not qualify as growth companies according to our criteria and that indeed have not returned so impressive financial results as the average of the 30 Dow Jones Industrials. Now, comparison of market prices in relation to earnings reveals that financial return such as would be consistent with true growth was not the main thing investors were interested in, anyway. In fact, it shows that they were apparently more interested in glamor than in growth.

Keeping in mind that the Dow Jones Industrial Average at the end of 1955 was selling for 15.3 times the average of earnings in the 1953–1955 period, note three facts:

1. Only three of Anderson's 25 companies (National Steel, Johns-Manville, and Standard Oil of California) were selling at a price/earnings ratio lower than the Dow Jones average—proof of the upward pressure on prices exerted by investors. At the same time, while for a variety of reasons the three companies mentioned may have been low on glamor, as a group they showed average or better-than-average financial results!

2. General Motors, United States Steel, and Bethlehem Steel were also selling at less than 15 times 1953–1955 earnings at the end of 1955, although there is no question that the financial results of these three companies were outstandingly impressive.

3. Of Anderson's 25 companies, 12 were selling for more than 20 times 1953–1955 earnings, even though this group included companies with clearly subaverage financial results, such as Union Carbide and Carbon, Hercules Powder, and Continental Oil.

To be sure, there are cases where the market price of the stock in relation to earnings is in line with its true growth characteristics. Thus, Scott Paper, Du Pont, IBM, and Dow Chemical, which happen to be the most expensive companies of our list of 33, do appear well qualified for their exalted price/earnings ratios of more than 30 times 1953–1955 average earnings; they clearly meet our qualitative criteria, and their financial results are well above average by any standard of measurement. But in many other cases investors have pushed the price far above what is justified not only in terms of current earnings but in terms of growth potential as well.

From the mass of contradictory evidence available, is it possible for the investor to find some guide or benchmark in his search for value? How can he make a choice among a group of such outstanding companies with such widely dispersed price/earnings ratios? How can he decide whether General Motors at 14 times 1953–1955 earnings is a better buy than Dow Chemical at nearly 40 times, or whether it is worth paying nearly twice as much for a dollar's worth of General Electric's earnings as for a dollar's worth of Westinghouse's?

There is a possible basis for answering these questions, but it involves a rejection of the conventional ratio of price to earnings as a measure of value. While the method to be proposed, even if accepted by the investing public, would hardly go so far as to shift the main focus of market interest from growth stocks to growth companies, it might well be used by the managements of undervalued growth companies as an effective tool in gaining more recognition from investors.

The Feel of the Market

There are two parts to this task of selecting stocks for future appreciation. The investor must satisfy himself (1) that the company is likely to continue to grow in earning power, and (2) that the stock is priced relatively low enough at time of purchase so the increase in earning power has a good chance to be reflected in greater value to the holder.

The first part we have, of course, already discussed in terms of qualitative analysis of the company (*not* the stock); a consistent upward trend in earnings and dividends, with the greatest possible potential based on dynamic management and supported by relative immunity to business fluctuations, should certainly indicate the prospects for continued growth in earning power.

The second part, which is our concern at this point, involves statistical analysis of the market price of the stock to determine whether it is a good buy in the sense of not being valued so high that in effect the results of future growth are already discounted (as so often happens when stocks become glamorized, particularly so-called growth stocks that do not have the characteristics of true growth to back them up).

But if the investor simply looks to see whether the stock is cheap or expensive on the basis of how many times earnings it is selling for, he ignores the primary consideration in his search—the discovery of growth. Earnings in any given period of time are a static concept. They are therefore only partly relevant to the valuation of growth companies. What the investor should look at is the *change* in earning power between two periods of time.

Accordingly, my suggestion is that the ratio of price to *increase* in earnings may be more significant than the conventional ratio of price to earnings. Investment requires a look into the future; intelligent appraisal of the future must be based on developing trends already in action and ascertainable; and this is one way of doing it. For example:

Let us take two fictional stocks, the Deadhead Company selling for $20, and the Zoomar Company selling for $30. If they are both currently earning $2 a share, Deadhead is selling for 10 times earnings and certainly looks cheaper than Zoomar, which is selling for 15 times. But if five years ago Deadhead's earnings were $1.60 while Zoomar was earning only $1.00, Deadhead's price is 50 times its $0.40-a-share increase-in-earnings, while Zoomar's price is only 30 times its $1.00-a-share increase-in-earnings. Now Zoomar clearly seems like the better value.

If the investor believes that the two companies will continue to grow in the future at about the same rates they showed in the past, there is no question that Zoomar is cheaper. Five years hence Zoomar will again have doubled its earnings and will be making $4 a share; thus its present price of $30 is only 7.5 times its future earnings. Deadhead, on the other hand, will be earning only $2.50 five years from now, so its present price of $20 is eight times its future earnings.

The ratio of price to increase-in-earnings makes some stocks look cheaper and some more expensive than the values indicated by the more conventional price/earnings measurement, as Table 1 shows. (The figures are presented for illustrative purposes only. In any serious application of the method, it would naturally be wise to examine the increase-in-earnings records for any windfalls—large one-shot government contracts, and so forth—and make any adjustments deemed necessary.)

Indeed, Table 1 shows clearly that the investor gets a wholly different slant on matters if he uses the ratio

Table 1   Price/Earnings-Increase Ratios of 10 Stocks

	End-of-1955 Price as a Multiple Of	
	1953–1955 Earnings	Increase-in-Earnings 1947–1949 to 1953–1955
IBM	36.5 ×	99 ×
Du Pont	32.3	61
Scott Paper	30.4	59
National Lead	26.4	41
Corning Glass	28.4	38
Hartford Fire Insurance	17.3	640
Continental Oil	22.6	550
J. C. Penney	18.7	382
Humble Oil	24.2	210
Union Carbide	28.6	159
Dow Jones Industrial Average	*15.3*	*53*

of price to increase-in-earnings rather than the more conventional ratio; the companies with superior financial results almost always appear to be more attractively priced on the new basis—notably, for instance, National Lead and Corning Glass. But it is also worth noting that, as Table 2 illustrates, some stocks were cheap at the end of 1955 by both standards of measurement—the explanation probably being that these are stocks where the glamor factor is relatively low, and thus the refinement of our method makes less difference.

In short, the price to increase-in-earnings ratio does serve to produce a different and presumably a truer, or at least more helpful, picture when the market is running

Table 2   Stocks Undervalued on the Basis of Both Price/ Earnings and Price/Earnings-Increase Ratios

	12/31/55 Price as a Multiple Of	
	1953–1955 Earnings	Increase-in-Earnings 1947–1949 to 1953–1955
Bethlehem Steel	11.0 ×	24 ×
U.S. Steel	12.9	25
General Motors	14.5	31
Standard Oil of California	13.5	39
Standard Oil of New Jersey	15.8	42
Johns-Manville	14.3	51
U.S. Gypsum	16.3	51

ahead of growth in earning power, yet at the same time it causes no distortion when the opposite is the case.

Now, how effective in actual practice is the increase-in-earnings ratio as the second part of our method for selecting stocks for future appreciation—in other words, for determining whether the stock of a growth company is also a good buy for this purpose in terms of current market price?

A test based on data for our sample of 33 companies at the end of 1952 reveals rather impressive results. To give expression to the first part of our method, the sample was combed out to select those companies with the most consistent records of rising earnings and dividends and with the best record of maintaining or increasing return on net worth. From this group, the five companies with the lowest and the five companies with the highest ratios of price to increase-in-earnings—in other words, the five cheapest and five most expensive stocks—were chosen as if for purchase. What the results would have been as of the end of 1955 are compared in Table 3 (the companies are listed in ascending order of their price to increase-in-earnings ratios at the end of 1952).

Although this test is based on a relatively short time period with plenty of peculiarities, the results are highly consistent. It may be seen that as a group the cheapest companies in terms of the ratio of price to increase-in-earnings far outperformed the most expensive ones. It is also significant that all five of the cheapest companies

Table 3   Price to Increase-in-Earnings Ratio Applied

	Percentage Increase in Price 12/31/52 to 12/31/55
FIVE CHEAPEST COMPANIES IN 1952	
Bethlehem Steel	221%
U.S. Steel	183
General Motors	108
Libbey-Owens-Ford	114
Standard Oil of New Jersey	96
Average	114
FIVE MOST EXPENSIVE COMPANIES IN 1952	
National Lead	160%
Westinghouse	25
Dow Chemical	45
Amerada	0
IBM	116
Average	69
Dow Jones Industrial Average	*65*

went up by more than the Dow Jones Industrials, while three of the expensive companies turned in very poor results.

Of course, there also are a few stocks of companies on the list that fail to meet the qualitative criteria of growth and yet show appreciation like the stocks of the best growth companies. This simply emphasizes the fact that no statistical analysis is perfect or self-sufficient, and that inspection of the individual situation must always be brought into the decision to buy a stock. But at least this approach is far more fruitful than simply purchasing so-called growth stocks. Indeed, Anderson's own data prove this point. His 25 income stocks outperformed his 25 growth stocks from 1936 through 1945. For the entire period he reviews—1936 through 1954—his growth stocks were outperformed as a group by such "non-growth" stocks as Goodyear, Bethlehem Steel, Beatrice Foods, and Truax-Traer Coal.

Here is one moral. In investing, nothing beats the discovery of an undervalued stock, no matter what the nature of its business or the past trend of its earnings. But simply purchasing so-called growth stocks tends to lead to the selection of overvalued stocks.

Furthermore, investors cannot wholly ignore the very low income return on most growth stocks—particularly institutional investors with little or no income tax to pay. The annual income on Anderson's 25 growth stocks did not catch up to that on his income stocks for 12 years or to the Dow Jones Industrials for 14 years. By the end of 1954, the entire amount of income received on the growth stocks from the beginning of 1936 was still less than on the income stocks or the Dow Jones Industrials.

Or look at it this way. In 1955, the dividend on the Dow Jones Industrials was equal to 10.2 percent of the price at the end of 1947. On General Motors it was 23 percent, on Bethlehem Steel 24 percent, and on National Lead

26 percent. But on 17 of Anderson's 25 growth companies it was less than 10 percent and three were actually yielding less than 6 percent on the 1947 price.

Thus, for those investors who can reinvest and compound income and for those who require a relatively high income, the very high premiums that some supposed growth stocks command may turn out to be less than worthwhile, even if satisfactory price appreciation results. For analysis proves that both appreciation *and* a large income can be realized with proper selection—that is, selection of true growth companies with a relatively low ratio of price to increase-in-earnings.

The magic words "growth company" are high praise in the business world today. It is perfectly proper for the spotlight to focus on those companies that are either making a significant contribution to or benefiting greatly from the vigorous growth patterns of our modern economy. But in order to avoid dangerous oversimplifications and in order to apply the term *growth company* only where it has some useful meaning, the following three considerations should be borne in mind:

1. Growth is a dynamic concept. The growth company can never be a passive beneficiary of economic change. Rather it must be an active agent at the technological or geographical frontiers of our society. Thus, it is not enough to be in, say, the chemical or

electronic industries; a firm cannot become a growth company by association. There may be more elements of growth (i.e., market creation) in a company like General Motors than in many chemical or electronics companies.

2. It is a mistake to believe that superior earning power is to be found only among growth companies, but it is a very decisive test for all such firms. Creativity and ambition in product development and merchandising alone are not enough; the ability to make money out of creativity is certainly at least as important.

3. The enchantment that some growth companies convey to the stock market lends a premium to their common stocks that is not always justified by the statistical background. An investor may do well with such stocks but there is good reason to believe that he can do even better by giving the financial results—such as those shown by measures of increase in earnings power—a completely cold-blooded and objective analysis. No amount of study in this area can minimize the importance of trying to buy at a fair price; buying at any price and hoping that the future will take care of itself is a good shortcut to disappointing results.

Indeed, perhaps the most important conclusion of this analysis is that the term *growth stock* is meaningless; a growth stock can be identified only with hindsight—it is simply a stock that went way up. But the concept of "growth company" can be used to identify the most creative, most imaginative management groups; and if, in addition, their stocks are valued at a reasonable ratio to their increase in earnings power over a period of time, the odds are favorable for appreciation in the future.

Chapter 3

INFLATION AND THE ECONOMY

Inflation has been the most overworked word in the American vocabulary for the past 25 years. While we have had several intense and unpleasant bouts with inflation since the end of World War II, prices have, in fact, gone up a good deal less and much more slowly than most casual conversations on the subject would lead you to believe. Furthermore, history tells us that the American economy has few, if any, inherent inflationary tendencies (or at least that it has strong counterinflationary forces) during *peacetime* periods.

The essays that follow try to bring these inflationary episodes into perspective and to stress their temporary character. The first three essays span the years from 1958 to 1964, when talk about inflation was persistent and when inflation was made the key reason to buy common stocks, but when, in fact, the increase in the cost of living averaged only a bit more than 1 percent a year. The third of these three, "Inflation and Stock Prices: A Jumble of Myths," dated December 1, 1964, deals not only with the relationship between inflation and common stocks, but also is a poignant reminder of what life was like before the escalation of the Vietnam war fundamentally disrupted an extended period of noninflationary economic growth. The last three essays in this chapter reveal further the unfortunate economic consequences of the decision to throw so much of our resources into Vietnam and then to postpone for so long the hard choice of how to finance this tragic adventure.

The essays also reveal a number of important paradoxes that fly in the face of conventional wisdom. Thus, we find no automatic or simplistic relationship between inflation and the state of the federal government's budget. Deficits in the balance of payments also seem to come and go without any particular relevance to what is happening to our domestic price trends. Most important of all from an investment standpoint, the available evidence suggests that, by and large, common stocks are a poor hedge against inflation.

Of course, it is easy to look back over a long span of years and to conclude that stocks have been a good hedge against inflation because both stock prices and the cost of living have risen over the long run. But this is a dangerously misleading conclusion.

Inflation and the Economy

In the first place, a statistical *association* between two series proves nothing about causality. For example, most people who drink milk in their early years tend to live longer than those who are deprived of it, which means that they are probably going to live long enough to die of cancer, heart trouble, and other types of degenerative diseases. Does this prove that milk *causes* heart trouble and cancer? In the same way, we are unable simply to look at parallel rising paths in the history of stock prices and the cost of living and to conclude that the increase in the cost of living made the stock market go up. Indeed, we could just as well argue the opposite case.

Second, and even more important, a more careful study of the long-run pattern shows that stock prices have gone up almost regardless of what has been happening in the cost of living. In fact, over most of the last hundred years and most particularly in the years since 1945, stocks have been a much better holding when the cost of living was moving in a generally horizontal position than when inflation was operating in full force. As the essays argue repeatedly, inflation tends to be a bearish rather than a bullish influence on stock prices. This means you should stay out of the market when you are concerned about inflation, rather than rush into it. We may *want* to own assets that appreciate in value when inflation strikes, but (1) we really want to hold such assets all the time anyway, and (2) there is no automatic directional signal that will tell us where to find them.

Thus, this group of articles, perhaps more than any of the others in this book, sets forth my basic thesis that the conventional wisdom you hear is likely to be wrong; if predicting the stock market and the economy were as delightfully easy as others make it sound, we would all be rolling in wealth.

INFLATION-MONGERING*

Recently some people were afraid that the country would be talked into a depression. Now there is a far greater danger: We stand a good chance of being talked into a major inflation.

There is nothing inevitable about inflation in the United States. On the contrary, strong deflationary influences are still very much with us. The basic economic forces that might counter inflationary pressures have lost none of their strength. But inflation is more than a matter of economic theory and arithmetic: It is ultimately a product of psychological moods and motivation. Loose talk, vituperative political accusations, and the almost reflex-action conviction of inevitable inflation can go a long way toward breaking down the powerful obstacles that still bar the path toward a cumulative upward price movement.

At a time when the conviction of inevitable inflation is gaining adherents daily, we believe that every

---

* A Bernstein-Macaulay bulletin, December 1, 1958.

patriotic citizen will want to be reminded of the strong counterinflationary forces that still remain to protect the much-maligned purchasing power of the dollar.

We confess at once to being a little repetitious. But the proponents of the inevitable inflation have led so many people to react without thinking that we must try hard to create new habits of reacting to economic facts.

First, the long-run price history of the United States gives little or no evidence of this so-called long-term inflationary trend. Since 1802, the average annual compounded rate of increase in the level of wholesale prices is only about one-half of 1 percent. In peacetime, the trend has been unmistakably downward, only wars leading to substantial price rises.

During World War II, the usual price inflation was suppressed by intricate price and rationing controls, but this only postponed the war-induced inflation to the time when controls were removed, so that wholesale prices jumped 50 percent from 1945 to 1948. Since 1948, however, the rise in the wholesale-price index has been only 14 percent—less than 1.5 percent a year. Significantly, more than three-quarters of this so-called inflation occurred during 1951, in connection with the Korean War.

Anyone who projects these facts into the conviction that the long-term price trend in the United States is upward has hardly given the truth very serious or objective attention.

Second, we must consider the pressures upon the wage level, which have clearly had a lot to do with the behavior of prices since the war. As a result of the very low birth rates of the late 1920s and the depressed years of the 1930s, the number of people of working age has grown since 1945 at a very slow rate. Meanwhile, the rising birth rate and the declining death rate have greatly increased the size of the nonworking population. Naturally, we have suffered from a labor shortage as a result. Now this situation is about to be dramatically reversed, as the war babies reach maturity. Between 1940 and 1950, the age group 20 to 64 grew by eight million; by 1960 only 6.7 million more will have been added. Between 1960 and 1970, however, this group will have grown by more than 12 million! Most of these will be young people in the 20 to 44 age bracket.

Is it logical to expect that wages will push up as rapidly under these conditions as they did when labor was in such desperately short supply? We believe that the worst of wage inflation is definitely behind us.

Third, support of a rising price level essentially requires money. And money is not nearly so plentiful as it was in the 1945–1955 period relative to the volume of business activity. The supply of money, as measured by the total of checking accounts and currency outside banks, was about $102 billion at the end of 1945; it had risen to $138 billion by the end of 1957. At the same time, however, the gross national product, which measures the dollar value of the total output of goods and services, rose from $213 billion in 1945 to $440 billion in 1957. Clearly, there has been a significant shrinkage in the liquidity that so readily financed the price rise of the earlier postwar years.

Limitations on the supply of money, strongly reinforced by the persistent (and occasionally even stubborn) attitude of the Federal Reserve people toward the need of fighting inflation can together go a long way to restrict a general increase in the price level.

Most important of all, the further one moves away from the security markets, the less inflation seems to be a factor in consumer and business decision-making.

Are businessmen building plants way in advance of their needs today, in order to avoid paying more for such plants in future years? Are they hoarding machinery and machine tools for fear that this equipment will cost so much more in 1960 or 1962? Are they relentlessly accumulating inventory well in excess of current output requirements, in order to beat the gun on increases in raw-material prices? Is the howl that has gone up for tariff protection, subsidies, import quotas, and so forth, symptomatic of a fear of rising prices in the United States?

The answer to these questions is obviously NO.

Are consumers stocking up on clothing, canned goods, appliances, automobiles, and toys today so that they can avoid paying more tomorrow? Are price increases stimulating consumers to expect further price increases and therefore intensifying their buying? Does the 20 percent increase in savings deposits since the end of 1956 represent a flight away from the dollar?

The answer to these questions is obviously NO.

No, despite all the chatter on the subject, neither business-men nor consumers have as yet accepted the inevitability of infla-tion. On the contrary, they cling to their dollars and give every indication of strong resistance to higher prices.

Only in Wall Street—and the telephone lines that feed into it—is inflation a dominant motivation in decision-making, although Washington is also becoming a breeding ground of the inflation obsession. And it is in this context that the danger lies. If the action of the stock market and the bond market, together with the alarmist cries from people in high places, begin to convince consumers and busi-nessmen that their normal conservative policies and respect for dollars are wrong, then we will be in for real trouble. Then none of the counterinflationary influences can stem the tide. Then the dollar will truly collapse.

But the point of the whole matter is that there is only a flimsy basis for believing that inflation is inevitable, and the forces opposing it can turn out to be as strong as or stronger than the forces that strengthen its potential. Consumer and business psychology are fragile, however, and subject to extremes in fads and emotional reactions. The more the facts are obscured, the greater the danger of a change in psychology.

We continue to hope that most Americans are too sensible to be panicked. Yet we also hope that they will do their buying in the stock market as rationally as they do their buying in the shops: with an eye to value and discrimination, and a belief in the reality and value of the dollar.

What Happened Afterward:

From the end of 1958 to the end of 1964, before the Vietnam escalation in 1965, the consumer-price index rose by only 7 percent altogether—only slightly more than 1 percent a year.

DEFICITS AND INFLATION: AN ANALYSIS OF THE INTERRELATIONSHIPS*

The most casual reading of the financial press—and of a good deal of Congressional oratory—reveals a widespread conviction that a federal deficit will automatically lead to an inflation of the price level. While observers may disagree as to whether this would be a desirable or undesirable consequence, we find surprisingly little disagreement over the supposedly direct cause-and-effect relationship between government deficits and an upward trend in the prices of goods and services.

Unfortunately, nothing is that simple. If it were, the art of prediction would be far less challenging. The link between federal deficits and the price level is neither direct

---

* A Bernstein-Macaulay bulletin, April 1, 1963.

nor automatic. In many instances, no relationship exists at all; to the extent that we can find a cause-and-effect relationship, the implications are rather different from what most people usually expect. Our intention here is to show how a deficit may—or may not—influence the prices that we have to pay for the goods and services that we buy.

Except during (or immediately following) World War II, when enormous debt-financed government expenditures drained the civilian sectors of the economy and when production was pushed to maximum limits, recent American history shows absolutely no systematic relationship between changes in the cost of living and federal government finances.

Prices rose despite federal surpluses in 1946–1948, 1950–1951, 1956–1957, and 1960. On the other hand, prices fell in 1949 despite a federal deficit. Large deficits in 1953 and 1954 were accompanied by negligible upward price movements. The increase in prices during the surplus year of 1957 was larger than during the deficit year of 1958. And, although 1958 saw our largest peacetime deficit, it has been followed by more than four years of relative price stability (and three more annual deficits).

Some additional history is significant. From 1897 to 1913, the rise in prices in the United States was twice as rapid as it was from 1948 to 1962. Yet the government ran a surplus in seven of these 16 years, and the national debt in 1913 was lower than it had been in 1897. Furthermore, the country was on a full gold standard at that time, so that the most conservative of monetary techniques was in use. What this suggests, in short, is that there is more to the causes of inflation than a federal deficit or easy monetary policies. As we stated at the outset: Nothing is that simple.

Inflation is a self-perpetuating rise in prices. Prices are determined by supply and demand. Prices increase when demand expands faster than output can be increased. Admittedly, demand will rise if government spending increases faster than tax receipts, or if taxes are cut more deeply than government spending. But the knowledge that demand is expanding is an insufficient basis for predicting inflation: we must also know whether enough labor and resources are available so that supply can keep pace with the growth in demand.

The error that many people make is to confuse a situation (such as wartime) where the supply of civilian goods cannot be expanded when demand is rising, with the fundamentally different situation in which labor and resources languish because demand is inadequate. This is the very problem that Americans are now facing: How can we stimulate enough demand to buy all the things that we are capable of producing? If the prescription for too much demand relative to supply is higher taxes or lower government spending, the same prescription can hardly be appropriate for an illness whose cause and symptoms are so diametrically opposed.

If inflation is ultimately a matter of supply versus demand, then *any* increase in demand, regardless of source, can lead to inflation *if* our productive capabilities are fully employed. Inflation could occur, therefore, even without a reduction in taxes, if businessmen started a big investment boom or if consumers went on an active spending spree. In other words, the financing of the expenditure is only indirectly related to the inflationary consequences: The crucial and central consideration is the relationship between demand and supply, between expenditure and production, between order backlogs and output schedules.

This is clearly illustrated by the experience of 1956–1957, when the economy had little excess capacity or idle labor available to expand output. Prices rose 5 percent over this two-year period. Was this the result of red figures in Washington? On the contrary, the surplus was $5.7 billion in 1956 and $2 billion in 1957. The rest of the economy, however, was rapidly increasing its expenditures, especially in the business sector. Business outlays on investment projects exceeded depreciation accruals and retained earnings by $45 billion in those two years. Thus, while government was actually repressing purchasing power by taking in more in taxes than it paid out, prices rose nevertheless because of a private "deficit-spending" inflation.

The 1956–1957 experience is significant in another connection. The price inflation it induced was short-lived despite repeated federal deficits since 1957. Except under the extraordinary pressures of war, supply seldom lags far behind demand in this fabulously productive economy of ours. Price increases rapidly lead to expanding production schedules and soon afterward to price stability or even price weakness. This has, in fact, been the major problem with which businessmen have been wrestling in recent years.

Thus, the relationship between government deficits and inflation is more coincidental than automatic. Inflation is always a problem where an economy is fully employed. It has no more than academic interest when the economy has as much slack as we now have in the form of idle plants and idle workers.

Rather, the danger we face is that an obsession with inflation will stand in the way of our taking the steps so urgently necessary to stimulate growth in production and employment. Timid businessmen, cautious consumers, inadequate profits, labor intransigence—all these are symptoms of too little business activity rather than too much. If inflation should develop, we have methods of containing it—and, in our economy, it tends to be self-curing in any case. But if production and employment continue to lag so far behind their potentials, we stand in real danger of collapsing under our own weight.

What Happened Afterward:

From the spring of 1963, when this bulletin was written, until the end of 1965, when the Vietnam escalation really took hold on the economy, the consumer-price index increased at an annual rate of less than 2 percent, even though the budget deficit in fiscal 1964 amounted to almost $6 billion.

INFLATION AND STOCK PRICES: A JUMBLE OF MYTHS*

Inflation has once again become a favorite topic of conversation. This is the result of a combination of influences: the wage settlements in Detroit, higher prices for nonferrous metals, the tax cut, wide upward price movements in Europe, and, just because that's the way people are, the sheer force of habits of thought.

Readers of these letters must know that for many years we have minimized the likelihood of widespread and rapid price increases in the American economy. We have also stressed that rising prices would have a less favorable influence on the stock market than relatively stable prices would have. The facts of history have justified this position, for the cost of living over the past 10 years has risen at the rate of only 1.1 percent a year while stock prices have much more than doubled over the decade.

We continue to believe that the inflation talk is overdone, especially in view of the recent action by the monetary authorities here and abroad. Furthermore, we continue to believe that a broad and accelerated increase in

---

* A Bernstein–Macaulay bulletin, December 1, 1964.

the prices of goods and services would be a reason to *sell* common stocks, not to buy them.

Any businessman who knows what he is doing (a few in high places admittedly don't) will refrain from raising his prices if his customers are unwilling or unable to pay more for his products, or if competitors who sell at lower prices can take his customers away from him. Thus, prices rise only when demand is vigorous and when the output of urgently wanted goods cannot be met by competing producers or by substitutes.

In recent years, despite expanding demands that were helped along by the tax cut, prices have been stable in many areas and have even declined in such important industries as chemicals, tires, electrical equipment, gasoline, and paper. The reason, of course, has been the pressure of competition from abroad as well as at home, excess capacity, and the American businessman's superb genius for making something better and cheaper to take business away from a competitor. In addition, wage rates have risen relatively slowly while productivity has advanced rapidly; this has provided businessmen with a continuously declining cost of labor per unit of output.

We see no reason to expect any material change in these conditions. The expansion of productive capacity, with emphasis on efficiency and cost reduction, has been proceeding at a rapid pace. Plant and equipment expenditures during 1962–1964 totaled $120 billion, compared with only $102 billion in the preceding three years.

Outlays in 1965 alone are expected to exceed $46 billion. Thus, the pressures of competition from expanded capacity combined with the continued introduction of labor-saving equipment are likely to prevent most business managements from raising prices, or at least from raising them enough to justify the tag of inflation.

At the same time, demand, although still expanding, may rise at a slower pace. The most reliable estimates for 1965 suggest an increase in the demand for goods and services little more than half as rapid as the increase we will score this year. In particular, the stimulus to lower- and middle-income families from the tax cut will be blunted both by under-withholding during 1964 and by the heavy load of installment-debt repayments now running at an annual rate of more than $60 billion—almost 14 percent of personal incomes after taxes. The eagerness of the Federal Reserve to clamp down on the supply of money will be another factor inhibiting demand.

These data suggest increasing resistance to higher prices. Thus, prices may fail to rise at all, or, if they do, sales may shrink, followed by a curtailment in production and employment. Either way, the consequence for profits would be bearish. This is primarily why we would consider inflationary symptoms a signal to sell common stocks rather than to buy them. But we think it also means that most industries will be less generous than the automobile people in their wage settlements: If this, in fact, turns out to be the case, we would expect the business upswing to have a better chance of continuing, because of greater stability of prices and profit margins.

We insist, in fact, that one can find much better reasons than inflation to justify the purchase of common stocks and that, indeed, inflationary periods have frequently been bad times to own common stocks. Yet most people continue to believe strongly that they *have* to buy common stocks to beat inflation. For this reason we are going to review the picture since 1946 once again:

- During the six years in the 1946–1964 period in which the consumer-price index rose by 3 percent or more, stock prices increased at an annual average rate of only 4.3 percent.
- During the 13 years in which the consumer-price index rose by less than 3 percent, stock prices increased at an annual average rate of 12.5 percent—almost three times as fast as under more inflationary conditions.
- The year of the largest increase in the cost of living— 1947—was also the year of the largest decline in stock prices since the war. The year in which stock prices rose the most—1955—was one in which consumer prices were unchanged.
- The rise in the consumer-price index since 1953 has been only about one-third as great as it was during the postwar and Korean War inflation that spanned the years from 1945 to 1953; stock prices, however, have

risen nearly four times as much since 1953 as they rose from 1945 to 1953.

• Stock prices have in any case overdiscounted infla-tion: On the average, common stocks are selling for five times the 1945 level, while the cost of living has only doubled.

In brief, inflation does little to add to and possi-bly detracts from the fundamental attraction of common stocks as an investment, while stocks have clearly been an excellent investment over the past 10 years or so of rela-tive price stability.

But this is by no means only an American phenom-enon. A similar set of patterns emerges from an analysis of the intense inflation that has characterized the European economy over the past three years:

	Percentage Change	
	August 1964 Compared with 1961 Average	
	Cost of Living	Share Price
Italy	+20	−49
France	+13	−18
Netherlands	+13	− 8
Switzerland	+12	−31
United Kingdom	+12	+17
Belgium	+ 9	− 2
Germany	+ 9	−11
United States	+ 4	+24

Thus, nonflationary Americans have enjoyed a buoyant stock market, despite the 1962 interruption, while common stocks in inflationary Continental Europe have been a poor hedge indeed. As a matter of fact, the table shows that the two European countries with the most inflation were much worse places to hold common stocks than were the two European countries with the least inflation.

This is an impressive array of facts. Yet, they should come as no real surprise to the thoughtful student of economic forces. Inflation is positively bearish or at least less bullish than price stability for the stock market because of two factors:

1. Inflation leads to dislocations and distortions that ultimately result in a business bust. The likelihood is that the bigger the inflation, the bigger the bust.
2. The government, in an effort to avoid just such a catastrophe, will make money tight and interest rates high, will keep taxes up or even increase them, and, possibly, will impose direct controls of various sorts. All of this makes goods harder to sell and production more difficult to finance.

In sum, then, it is because of its ominous consequences for corporate earning power that inflation is a poor reason to buy common stocks. A slower expansion with a steady price level has the great advantage of postponing the speculative excesses that always mark the beginning of the end.

Our own view of 1965, in fact, is that the expansion of demand throughout the economy will be less than it was in 1964. Meanwhile, with so much new and efficient capacity coming onstream and with the size of the labor force increasing at an accelerated rate, we also see little or no upward pressure from costs. This would provide just the proper environment for the pattern of fiscal stimulation that the Administration is now beginning to discuss.

For all of these reasons, we think the odds favor a continued if subdued rise in business activity and, in many cases at least, an increase in corporate profits as well. On the other hand, however, we would counsel the sale of common stocks in the less likely event that inflationary pressures should intensify and persist, or if the authorities yield further to the temptation to invoke anti-inflationary measures prematurely.

What Happened Afterward:

Business continued strong, with growth well balanced, until the autumn of 1965. At that time, the escalation of Vietnam hostilities became the announced objective of the Johnson Administration, with a substantial increase in defense spending projected for the period ahead. The consumer-price index increased by almost 3 percent during 1966 and at an accelerating rate thereafter. Stock prices tumbled sharply between the end of 1965 and the autumn of 1966 and did not regain the late-1965 highs for almost two years. As inflation gathered momentum and was not even blunted by the tax surcharge passed during 1968, stock prices once again turned downward into the bear market of 1969. The strongest period of stock prices after the 1966 decline was during 1967, when economic growth was relatively slow in the aftermath of the money crunch of 1966.

Hence, the relationships discussed in this bulletin did not change in the following four and a half years. Inflation continued to be a bad time to be in the stock market.

INFLATION REVISITED*

Since everyone is an expert on inflation these days, we thought that our readers might enjoy trying their skill at a simple little quiz on the subject. The following is a multiple-choice type quiz, in which you choose in each case the correct answer from *A* or *B*:

WILL PRICES RISE MORE RAPIDLY . . .

1. When the demand for goods and services is expanding
    A. rapidly
    B. slowly
2. When unemployment is
    A. declining
    B. rising

---

* A Bernstein-Macaulay bulletin, September 1, 1966.

3. When the supply of money is growing
   A. rapidly
   B. slowly
4. When public and private debts are expanding
   A. rapidly
   B. slowly
5. When utilization of manufacturing capacity is
   A. high
   B. low
6. When manufacturers' unfilled orders are
   A. rising
   B. falling

If you answered *A* to all of the questions, you may consider yourself as having flunked with a zero score, for recent history indicates that the correct answer in each instance turns out to be *B*. This is shown by the following array of facts:

	Increase per Annum (%)	
	1957–1961	**1961–1965**
PRICE CHANGES MEASURED BY		
Consumer-price index	1.3	1.3
Implicit GNP deflator	1.8	1.5
ECONOMIC TRENDS		
Gross national product (current $)	3.6	6.7
Gross national product (1958 $)	2.3	5.2
Unemployment	12.9	−8.0
Money supply	1.7	3.6

	Increase per Annum (%)	
	1957–1961	1961–1965
Total debt outstanding	5.4	7.4
Average manufacturing capacity utilization	Falling	Rising
Unfilled orders of manufacturers	−2.5	7.4

Thus, inflation in the later period was no greater and, measured by the comprehensive GNP deflator, probably smaller than in the earlier period, *even though* during 1961–1965 demand was expanding more rapidly, unemployment was shrinking rather than rising, money supply and debt were growing faster, and utilization of manufacturing capacity and unfilled orders were rising rather than failing.

But the quiz has a second part: Do stock prices rise more rapidly when the cost of living is (*A*) rising rapidly, or (*B*) rising slowly? Once again the correct answer is B, although this is also contrary to what popular opinion believes. As we pointed out in great detail in an earlier bulletin (December 1, 1964) and as the *Wall Street Journal* also demonstrated in its issue of August 10, all of the big bull-market years since the end of World War II, with the sole exception of 1951, have been years in which the cost of living was steady or rose by a maximum of 1 percent.

The period of the largest increase in the cost of living, 1946–1948, saw stock prices rise only 5 percent; the period of the smallest increase in the cost of living, 1954–1956, saw stock prices rise 50 percent. All of this is confirmed by recent European experience, where the degree of price inflation has been three to four times as intense as our own and has been accompanied by prolonged and deep declines in the prices of common stocks.

This is, in short, a subject in which unsophisticated oversimplification is likely to be wrong and even positively dangerous. The causes and consequences of inflation are more complex and obscure than the average level of Wall Street conversation might suggest.

Yet, we may be able to uncover a possible, although by no means certain, solution to the riddle of why the prices of goods and services rose so much from 1957 to 1961 when the pressure of inflationary forces was so much less than it was from 1961 to 1965. The following little table should make this clear:

	Increase per Annum (%)	
	1957–1961	1961–1965
Hourly wage rates in manufacturing	3.2	2.7
Nonagricultural output per man-hour	1.8	3.3

Thus, with wages rising faster and productivity more slowly in the earlier period, the increase in labor cost per unit of output was obviously much greater than it was in the following four years. This provides another ironic twist: Who would have expected wages to go up more when unemployment was growing than when it was shrinking?

These data suggest other intriguing links among the various parts of the economic process. The combination of tax cuts (including the investment credit) and an expansionary monetary policy surely contributed to the more rapid growth in the demand for goods and services in the later period. This in turn created the proper environment for businessmen to be willing to take the risks of sinking more money into capital equipment, thereby leading in turn to greatly improved productivity. The consequent easing of the upward pressure of costs meant more stable prices—and this moderated the demands of the unions for higher wages.

In the present conjuncture of events, a fundamental inflationary condition is intensified by an increasingly militant stand on the part of the unions. This is only in part a result of the somewhat more rapid rise in living costs in recent months; it is due more to the bulging levels of corporate profits that developed out of the 1961–1965 experience. The ditching of the guidelines is an ominous omen of things to come, in which wages and prices may once again move up under conditions of slower economic growth, as they did during the 1957–1961 period. Indeed, the dangers in a too restrictive fiscal or monetary policy lie precisely in discouraging businessmen from making the capital investments that are so essential to cost reduction and productivity improvements.

Experience and logic both tell us that the current atmosphere is hardly one in which the common stocks of basic industrial companies can move back up to their old highs. The hedges against inflation must be found among those companies where inflation has least to do with their fortunes—and this is, in fact, the pattern that the stock market has traced this year, through good months and bad.

That makes the investor's task more complicated. But the point of this essay was to demonstrate the unhappy truth that nothing is simple in this world!

What Happened Afterward:

The Dow Jones Industrial Average, which represents the stocks of the big, basic industrial companies in our economy, never regained its early-1966 high in the market recovery that followed the publication of this bulletin. On the other hand, stocks of growth companies, technological leaders, emerging small companies, and special situations—all unrelated to inflation—scored tremendous gains over the next two years.

CAN—AND SHOULD—TAXES STOP INFLATION?*

The passion and zeal with which the Administration has been advocating the income-tax surcharge seems to be

* A Bernstein-Macaulay bulletin, March 1, 1968.

matched only by the apparent indifference of the rest of the country as to whether it is passed or not.

The President and Mr. Fowler argue, with remarkable consistency to be sure, that the income-tax surcharge is essential to snuff out the fires of inflation that are already lit and that threaten soon to become a raging inferno beyond control. Yet, those economists who use the most comprehensive and sophisticated econometric models for business forecasts disagree: Their projections indicate that the tax increase will have little, if any, impact upon the projected increase in commodity prices and the cost of living.

Why do these models arrive at such a paradoxical conclusion and what insight into the future do they provide for us?

The most widely held basis for disbelief in the effectiveness of the tax surcharge as an anti-inflationary device is the strong expectation that cost-push—that is, wage increases in excess of productivity—will press upward on prices no matter what happens to the consumer's take-home pay or to corporate profits after taxes, or, indeed, to the level of government spending and the state of the national budget.

The argument has a good deal of merit. Our postwar history suggests that these episodes of rising prices have a certain inevitability about them and that they will persist until fundamental countervailing forces finally suppress them. The sequence of events, however, is somewhat different from what we might logically expect to see.

The chart on the facing page shows the major swings since 1948 in profits, prices of manufactured commodities, and the relation between labor costs and output in manufacturing. The vertical dotted lines connect the major low points of the two upper series with the line charted below each of them and help the eye to identify the leads and the lags.

The pattern is clear enough. Instead of labor costs pushing prices up, what we see instead is a sort of *profit*-push, for profits are already well on their way up before prices begin to rise and, indeed, prices are well on their way up before wages begin to rise faster than output. In other words, the forces set in motion by a significant surge in profits seem to lead to an episode of price inflation; this in turn leads labor to want to catch up to the rise in profits and living costs, so that the elements of profit-squeeze then appear upon the scene. Perhaps most important, the chart shows that labor costs per unit of output level out or decline only *after* prices have stopped rising, which means that a significant improvement in profitability must also await the snuffing out of inflationary pressures.

This is, of course, an oversimplification, for it omits many of the other factors at work. The 1957–1958 episode, for example, shows that a sharp rise in profits was followed by a rise in labor costs per unit of output but that no significant increase in prices intervened (was this perhaps because this episode was marked by the junior credit crunch of 1959?).

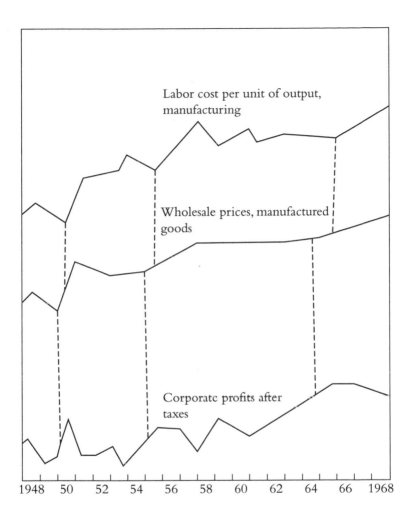

The basic patterns, however, seem beyond argument. By failing to ask for a tax increase in early 1966, *before* the rise in prices had really got under way, the Administration provided just enough time for the whole process to work itself out to the point at which we now find ourselves. Furthermore, they are themselves guilty of oversimplification in making a mechanical connection between budget deficit and price inflation: The sharp upswing in prices in 1950 occurred while the budget shifted from a deficit of about $5 billion to a surplus of nearly $20 billion, while the 1955–1957 episode occurred during an uninterrupted period of budget surpluses.

Of course, those who believe that monetary policy provides all the answers have their own brand of oversimplification. The money supply (including time deposits at commercial banks) rose by 3.6 percent during 1950; it rose by only 2.4 percent a year during 1955–1957; the monetary expansion in 1965 was a little faster than in the previous years but was much less in 1966. On the other hand, during the 1951–1954 period of price stability, the money supply grew at an average annual rate of 4.3 percent and at the remarkably high average annual figure of 7 percent from the end of 1959 to the end of 1965. Thus, we can find no basis for expecting price inflation to slow down if we cut back on the expansion in the money supply; on the contrary, we might expect the opposite to be the case.

When we have had enough of looking at numbers and interrelationships and try to sort out what we have seen, we find that we are faced with a set of disturbing paradoxes; profits seem to push prices and labor costs up rather than vice versa, and a significant rise in profits must await a flattening out of labor costs and prices. Furthermore, prices seem to be more stable when the economy enjoys the expansionary influences of monetary and fiscal policy than when more conservative policies prevail.

Our postwar history tells us that episodes of sharply rising prices tend to be short-lived, that supply rises to meet demand, that American businessmen are creative in offsetting rising labor costs, that productivity, expansion, and market creation are our great talents. This is the atmosphere we need. Hence, the dangers in repressing these factors could be greater than the dangers in an inflationary episode.

CAN WE SOCK IT TO THEM IN 1969 AS WE SOCKED IT TO THEM IN 1968?*

Despite the almost incredible horrors of assassination and violence that marred 1968, it was in many ways The Year of Happy Surprises.

Without warning, the President deescalated the war at the end of March and announced his decision not to run again. The international monetary system tottered twice on the very brink of collapse but ended the year still viable and functioning. Doubts about the self-discipline of

---

* A Bernstein–Macaulay bulletin, January 1, 1969.

Americans (particularly in an election year) were resolved when the income-tax surcharge passed, and doubts about the dangers of economic overkill were resolved when the surcharge appeared to be having too little rather than too much of an impact. Our ridiculous electoral system survived a crucial test that many feared it would fail. Even bondholders, as we predicted in our bulletin exactly one year ago, surprised most people by enjoying a happy new year for at least part of the time.

This was the pattern that suggested the question posed in our title. Are the surprises that lie ahead of us going to be as happy as the surprises of 1968? Except for the poor bondholder, once again mired in the slough of despond, most segments of the economy are looking forward to a rip-roaring 1969. If the past is any guide, this means that only the bondholder can have happy surprises; unlike last year, pleasant developments are already built into the expectations of everyone else and would therefore come as no surprise at all.

In a recent address, Sidney Homer of Salomon Brothers and Hutzler seemed to us to express most cogently our own doubts about the present conjuncture of events. He argues that the current package of expectations,

> great prosperity, accelerating inflation, rising credit demands, declining gold reserves, rising interest rates, falling bond prices, rising stock prices, and a growing preference of institutions to buy stocks . . . cannot continue indefinitely. This is because there

are serious reasons to suspect long-range incompatibilities which will at some point make the economy choose between one or another of these trends.

The whole problem is summed up in the deep demoralization of the bond market, reflecting as it does the urgent desires of investors of all types and sizes to own equities instead of fixed-dollar securities. There is, of course, some irony in watching institutions scorn bonds at yields of 7 percent or more when less than 15 years ago they were delighted to buy bonds under 4 percent and were scared to death of stocks yielding over 5 percent. While this shift in attitudes is, of course, a consequence of the economic environment of the past 15 years, and particularly the intensified inflationary atmosphere of the past three years, the real question is still the one posed by Mr. Homer: *Are inflation and a rising stock market compatible in the long run with a declining bond market?*

Here we must draw a crucial distinction. If bond buyers say, "We will continue to buy bonds, but only at a price lower than the present one," some kind of a bond market will still exist. If, however, they say, "We will never buy any more bonds, regardless of how low the price at which they are offered to us," no bond market exists. This is the great danger in the current revulsion from bonds: We will have only sellers and no buyers.

But in 1967, all but $2.9 billion out of a total of $68.5 billion of new security issues took the form of bonds!

Furthermore, $43.6 billion of the new bond issues were obligations of federal and local governments, which have no other source of external financing. But almost 90 percent of nonbank external financing by corporations took the form of bonds as well.

What this means, as a practical matter, is that the investor's flight from bonds is indeed incompatible with the continuation of an inflationary economy and a booming stock market.

Inflation means that the dollar value of the gross national product is rising faster than the physical growth in the output of goods and services. But that rising dollar value of output has to be financed, and the greater the inflation, the greater the financing requirements. If we effectively eliminate the bond market, our overwhelmingly major source of finance, then the dollar value of output is not going to rise. Turning on the tap of the money supply by increasing the loanable funds of the commercial banks will only intensify inflationary expectations and hasten the demise of the bond market. Ultimately, then, either output or prices must fall or, even worse, both will fall because of the blockage in financing capabilities.

Of course, we can finance an expanding dollar value of production without the bond market and the banks if we turn increasingly to equity financing or if we give bondholders what is so aptly termed an equity "sweetener." Inflation can then, in fact, continue, but it will be the bond market rather than the stock market that will be buoyant. It will be on the equity side that supply increases faster than demand. In other words, to repeat Mr. Homer's thesis, a rising stock market, a falling bond market, and price inflation are mutually incompatible: Something has to give.

If we have no bond market, inflation will probably turn into deflation for lack of financing. If we turn instead to the stock market for financing, inflation may continue, but stocks will turn out to be a very sour hedge indeed. We can have viable security markets, in fact, only if we can repress inflation before chaos sets in.

Thus, three choices lie ahead of us: (1) The bond market must begin to attract buyers somewhere near current levels, (2) the stock market will be depressed by a rush of new equity financing, or (3) the economy will go into a tailspin for lack of financing. No matter how you figure it, all three of these possibilities suggest that bonds (and stocks that move in sympathy with bond prices) may well be at a most interesting buying level at the present time, while more volatile stocks are much less attractive than they were a year ago.

The first possibility, which is surely the most attractive of the three, presumes some easing of inflationary expectations in the near future. That is the clear objective of the Federal Reserve and the Treasury right now. We are inclined to believe they will succeed, particularly if we can stop the war in Vietnam. Regardless of our beliefs, however, this is surely the necessary set of conditions for the happy 1969 we wish all of you.

What Happened Afterward:

Long-term interest rates rose sharply during the first three months of 1969; they then flattened out and drifted downward in the months that followed, even though short-term rates continued to move higher. The stock market, on the other hand, moved steadily downward during 1969, in part under the pressure of a heavy volume of new issues. New common-stock issues for the year 1969 ran to $7.7 billion, about double the level for the year 1968 and nearly four times as high as the volume issued in 1967. Convertible bonds issued for cash amounted to $4 billion and were 25 percent above 1968, only slightly below 1967, and more than double the 1966 level.

Thus, the unfriendly bond market resulted in a huge wave of equity financing that helped to depress the stock market—but ultimately took some of the pressure off the bond market so that bond prices leveled out. Once again, we had a demonstration of the "sour hedge" against inflation provided by the stock market.

INFLATION: THE WRONG MEDICINE*

Hang out the flags and sound the klaxons—the Great White Fathers in Washington have brought economic growth in the United States down to zero. It took a lot

---

* From the *Nation*, February 16, 1970.

of pulling and tugging to get us there, but they have finally won. They have administered the classic medicine of higher taxes and tight money and have cooled off the economy. The catalogue of their victories is impressive. Not only is real growth down to zero, but unemployment is up, housing is way down, profits are tightly squeezed, the stock market is a shambles, interest rates are at record highs, appropriations for education are curtailed, and even the military is left begging for a few crumbs.

The only trouble is that prices are also up. The cost of living rose 4.6 percent in 1968 and then, despite the tax surcharge and ever tighter monetary policy, it rose more than 5 percent in 1969. And there are no meaningful signs of a letup in the inflationary spiral. In recent weeks, prices of steel, copper, aluminum, and a variety of chemicals have been increased, to say nothing of transit fares, commuter fares, and state and local property and excise taxes. We were startled back in 1965 when wages started going up by 5 to 6 percent a year, but now the prevailing rate is closer to 10 percent.

In short, what doth it profit a man to smash the upward momentum of our great economy if he loseth the battle against inflation? Since we are possibly on the verge of an economic crisis, it is time to rethink policies and to ask whether there is still time for a change. It will not be enough just to reverse the old policies—those who are hesitant on that score have some valid arguments on their side: We also need *new* policies that can overcome inflation without at the same time tearing apart the entire fabric of our prosperity.

The theory behind the classic medicine for the treatment of inflationary diseases is simple and appealing. Prices go up because demand exceeds supply. Reduce demand, therefore, and prices will stop going up. Raise taxes, cut government spending, make business and consumer spending more difficult and expensive to finance. Businessmen will then find that with lower demand they are unable to sell everything they can produce; if they persist in raising prices, their competitors will steal their customers. Thus the overheating in the economy is reduced and the price level flattens out. The whole process is assisted by a slower pace of wage increases, as businessmen become a lot tougher about accepting higher costs when they are unable to pass them along so easily to their customers.

Of course, there are other ways to fight inflation, among them wage and price controls or voluntary guidelines (known as an "incomes policy" in European countries). But such policies, according to advocates of the classic medicine, interfere with the free play of market forces, produce artificial and unfavorable allocations of resources, and, since they are difficult to administer, invite violation.

But the trouble with the classic medicine of squeezing down demand is that it too can fail to work as it should. Ultimately, if prices continue to rise in the face of shrinking demands for goods and services, it seems pointless to press so hard on the economy that a depression results. Indeed, the heavy hand of fiscal conservatism and tight money fails on three counts.

First, these policies seem to place little or no restraint on those important sectors of the economy where, as the economists put it, demand is inelastic—that is, where the customer is either determined or forced to keep buying, regardless of price increases. This is particularly the case in the service industries where, because of the high labor content, inflation keeps rolling merrily along no matter what the authorities do about taxes and interest rates. The prices of consumer services other than rent have gone up more than 50 percent in the past 10 years; they rose more than 7 percent in 1969 alone, more than twice as fast as the cost of the goods that consumers buy (wholesale prices, incidentally, are up only 15 percent in 10 years). Subway and commuter fares, haircuts, domestic help, medical care, and laundry and cleaning are just a few examples of this phenomenon.

Ironically, the government's cost of living goes up faster than anything else. The prices of goods and services purchased by government are rising about 10 percent faster than the prices that consumers pay. Civil servants, police, firemen, teachers, garbage collectors, councilmen and Congressmen, and privates and generals are all demanding, and getting, more. No wonder, then, that state and municipal taxes keep going up, or that the President's

Spartan budget involves deep cuts in what many people would consider essential federal activities.

The second count on which the classic medicine fails to achieve its objective is in the allocation of resources. Those who believe that higher taxes and tight money leave the operation of free-market forces intact, and that they will therefore emerge from the period of rigor with a more desirable mix of output than they would have under price and wage controls, are looking at the world with blinders. It was not so serious in the mini-money crunch of 1959 to 1960 that housing construction fell off, because housing was not then in short supply. But the supply was growing shorter in 1966 when the industry was felled by a body blow from which it was barely recovering when the haymaker of 1969 was delivered. The housing shortage is now desperate from high-income areas to low, a scandalous blot on a supposedly affluent society. Meanwhile, with inflation pushing wage rates in construction steadily upward—and pushing at the same time on land costs and interest rates—the price of housing is rising at an alarming rate; indeed, the rising cost of this essential item is simply feeding inflationary pressures throughout the rest of the economy.

But it is not only housing that suffers from the classic medicine. If you reduce demand, you ultimately reduce supply. Lower levels of production mean higher unit costs and greater pressure to keep prices up. A tight enough squeeze leads business management to cut back on plans to expand productive capacity, so that, when the authorities finally do allow business activity to pick up again, shortages develop all over the place and new inflationary symptoms rapidly appear.

But these are not the only ways in which the administration of the classic medicine to the free market leads to an allocation of resources different from what we might want. Part of the prescription for this medicine calls for a reduction in government spending. Hence, between conscious budgetary decisions in Washington and virtually insoluble financing problems in state capitals, we are now cutting back on education, on scientific research, on manpower training, on housing, on medical aid to the poor, on aid to the cities, among other things. True, production is being cut back at the automobile factories, the television factories, the chemical factories, and the steel factories—but are the resources released there moving into education or housing or urban renewal? Of course not. They are moving into the lines of the unemployed.

The third and most disturbing count against the classic medicine, in addition to its failure to curtail price increases in the service areas and its inflationary and irrational impact on resource allocation, is the giant risks it takes in dealing with the inflationary mentality. For inflation is more than an excess of demand over supply; it is also a state of mind. Americans have learned this the hard way in the present inflationary episode because it is unique in our recent history. After World War II, although prices rose very sharply from 1946 to 1948, rapid conversion to peacetime production and the absorption of millions of ex-GIs into the labor force enabled supply to grow at an extraordinary rate and to overwhelm demand within three years. The pattern repeated itself after Korea. In 1957–1958, before the inflationary virus could really get into our veins, the classic medicine contributed to the deepest of our postwar recessions and then kept us below maximum growth rates for at least three years.

This time, the story has been different. First, prices had been remarkably stable all during the period of impressive economic growth that preceded the 1965 escalation in Vietnam, so that inflationary expectations were slow to get started even though prices soon started climbing at a disturbing rate. But President Johnson, for a variety of reasons, postponed too long the unattractive recommendation of a tax increase. The Federal Reserve jammed on the monetary brakes in 1966. Then, although the brakes really took hold and prices did flatten out (again, except in the service area), fear of overkill soon led to a relaxation of monetary policy. Easier money also accompanied the early months after passage of the tax increase in mid-1968.

These vacillations of policy, combined with a genuine condition of demand in excess of supply, finally convinced the American people that nothing would stop inflation and that now it was every man for himself. With the prices of everything climbing so fast, no union leader could afford to ask for a smaller wage increase than his competitors were winning. No businessman could wait too long to raise prices, for fear that he would never be able to keep pace with his costs and maintain his profit margin. The most serious and distressing aberration of the inflationary mentality also appeared in earnest: buy today because tomorrow it will cost more. This attitude has taken hold to some extent with consumers, but it has become endemic in the business community where, despite much excess capacity, high financing costs, and flat sales curves, spending for the expansion of plant and equipment has continued to climb. When the inflationary wave finally subsides, an incalculable amount of this expenditure will turn out to have been ill-timed and misplaced.

How can the authorities deal with this type of mentality, which keeps the inflationary spiral spinning and spinning? Only by putting on the screws, tightening them continuously, and stubbornly keeping them tight regardless of objective evidence that would otherwise justify a reversal of policy. In other words, the authorities must be Firm, Courageous, Determined. Any suggestion of a weakening in their resolve not only would make possible a renewal of actual inflationary forces but would show that they do not Mean Business. Consequently, they have to keep the screws on beyond any measure of doubt, beyond the point where inflation *might* be tapering off, until, in God's good time, the price level is finally moving up at only a nominal rate or, even better, moving sideways.

But that is precisely where the danger of overkill comes in. If, because of the dangers inherent in the persistence of inflationary expectations, the authorities dare not change policies too soon, they inevitably run the risks of changing them too late. Indeed, if any one policy, such as the tax surcharge, fails to act as expected, then other policies, such as tight money, must be laid on with extra vigor.

Hence we now stand at a point where the overall level of business activity has ceased its normal upward moment. But it is also a point where private debts are at record highs and the liquidity that businessmen and individuals sorely need is at record lows. By keeping the lid on the money supply for most of 1969, the authorities made financing of expenditures increasingly difficult, so that every possible source of cash was tapped and liquid reserves in all areas were run down to virtually nothing. Consequently, as business activity tapers off, we have perilously little slack, too little margin for error. Only retrenchment down the line can rebuild the cash needed to pare these debts down. Under such circumstances, trouble in one spot can spread like a forest fire to another and another and another.

And yet, unless a really severe financial crisis erupts, the authorities will shift toward an easier stance only gradually, if at all. They are surely aware of the dilemma in which they have found themselves. But the grand strategy of the classic medicine has painted them into a corner; they simply don't know the way out.

The difficulties extend beyond this point. If all goes reasonably well, so that business activity does slow down a little and not too much, so that wage contract settlements are easier to make but without a heavy load of unemployment, so that price increases taper off but without a ruinous bout of price wars, so that people finally realize that inflation has been snuffed out but that economic growth is still "in"—if all of this happens, we might then begin to think once again in terms of a resumption of growth in production, of higher profits, or more employment, of more public spending for the educational facilities and hospitals and housing we need so urgently. *Or will we?*

If this reduction of the inflation fever occurs too soon, we shall have rebuilt too little liquidity to finance the increased spending that a resumption of growth implies. Money will be either too expensive to borrow or simply unavailable on any terms, but individuals and business firms will have insufficient cash to finance their expenditures without borrowing. If, as an offset, the Federal Reserve authorities allow the money supply to increase so that this financing bottleneck is broken, they run the very real risk that their policy will finance price increases as well as production increases—and that the public will read their decision as a belated but nonetheless significant capitulation to the insatiable monetary pressures of inflation.

Hence, even if we avoid recession or worse, the outlook for the resumption of economic growth in step with our potentialities is bleak. From 1957 to 1960, when similar attitudes prevailed and when the business recovery from the 1958 recession was aborted by supertight money in 1959, our output of goods and services rose a total of only 7.7 percent, compared with growth of 19.1 percent from 1960 to 1964, when less Calvinist philosophies prevailed.

And slow growth is no fun. It can lead to excessively high unemployment rates at a time when the labor force is rising rapidly as the postwar babies born in the 1940s and 1950s reach working age. In addition, the 800,000 or so people added to the armed forces as a result of the Vietnamese adventure will be going through demobilization and many of them will also be looking for work.

But slow growth implies more than the painful and shocking phenomenon of people who want work and cannot find it. Each percentage point of annual growth means about $10 billion worth of production, which is, for example, the equivalent of about 500,000 dwelling units or almost half again as much as total federal annual budget outlays on education and manpower. If we have zero growth during 1970 (let us hope we avoid an actual decline in total output), we shall have failed to produce at least $40 billion of goods and services that we have the capability of producing, much of which we could put to good use to improve the quality of life in this nation. Are we going to have a replay of the 1957–1960 experience, when production ran a total of nearly $100 billion, or around 20 percent below potential output over a three-year period?

Seen from this view, at this moment in time, the classic medicine may kill the patient before it cures him; at best, it may result in lingering side effects that will long delay a resurgence of robust good health. Yet, two years ago or so, when the argument about the tax surcharge was raging, most economists, regardless of political stripe or theoretical preferences, would have agreed that the classic medicine was the right thing to prescribe in the circumstances. What we failed to understand, or to foresee, was the virulence with which the inflationary mentality was going to take hold. It had not happened before: Despite all the talk about inflation ever since the war, very few instances of excessive forward buying or of charging every penny the market would bear could be found. Indeed, the remarkable price stability of the first five years of the decade in the face of rapid economic growth only fortified the impression that a little tight money and a little additional tax burden would relieve us of the problem in short order.

What we now know is that this approach cannot work in an atmosphere where people not only talk about inflation but *act* on it. Raise taxes, and consumers and businessmen will cut their savings or go into debt to maintain or increase their expenditures. Deny the commercial banks the resources to make loans or buy bonds, and they will dig deep and pay any price to find new ways to raise money to lend out. Their customers, meanwhile, will also tap new sources and pay any price for cash in order to spend today instead of tomorrow. Worse yet, a "gimme-gimme" mentality develops, in which everyone wants the highest possible price for his labor or goods or services in order to be able to pay the gouging high price that he expects to be charged on the things that he must buy. This process is completely self-generating and can continue almost indefinitely.

Under these circumstances, the authorities have no choice but to remain steadfast, to overstay and to gamble with the risk of overkill. But then this means that the classic medicine is no longer appropriate for the illness from which we suffer. In short, anyone who takes the most superficial look at the business statistics can see that we are no longer in a condition where demand exceeds supply, but wages and prices are still going up at an alarming rate. Hence, instead of squeezing demand still further (and squeezing it some more later on when it begins to pick up again), we now have no choice but to go after the inflationary process itself and do something *directly* about the price and wage situation.

It is true, of course, that controls are devilishly hard to administer, particularly in the absence of a great national motivation such as inspired the nation during World War II. In addition, any set of controls inevitably creates injustices and inequalities. This means that violations may be annoyingly frequent and that pressures to get out from under the controls may lead to their premature relaxation. Yet the risks here seem minor compared with the gigantic risks we run by continuing to administer the classic medicine. Furthermore, it is ironic that the moralistic Nixon Administration has so explicitly excluded any form of even informal and indirect influence on the wage and price decision-making process—no jawboning, no guidelines, no criticism of the greed that has taken hold and is widespread. Just cut spending and throw people out of work.

The direct way to make people stop trying to beat the price increases and to charge as much as (or even more than) the market will bear is to tell them that prices are going to stop going up or, at least, stop going up so fast. Let us return to a set of guidelines as to what is admissible and proper in raising prices and to what extent we can raise wages without pressing on prices. Let us put business and labor on the defensive when it comes to these decisions, instead of leaving them aggressively on the offensive.

There may be howls and grumbles and violations. But the American people are not stupid, and they are frightened about where the present process may be leading them. Tell John Jones that the cost of living will rise only 3 percent instead of 6 percent next year, and he will handle himself very differently. Tell him that his earnings will also go up more slowly—but that everyone's wage boosts are also going to slow down, and he will take it in stride. *When he stops expecting inflation, he will stop helping to create inflation.* And when we stop expecting inflation, the distortions and tensions in our financial markets will also begin to unwind, relieving the terrible and imminent dangers of a crisis there.

President Nixon has always seemed to be much more a pragmatist than a man who adheres rigidly to doctrine. Arthur Burns, new chairman of the Federal Reserve Board, is reputed to have a similar temperament. They have very little time left in which to prove that this is so.

Chapter 4

GOLD AND THE BALANCE OF PAYMENTS

To those of us who reached maturity during the 1930s and 1940s, the deteriorating international position of the dollar that began in the late 1950s has been a singularly traumatic experience. In the years before World War II, we saw the gold pour into our coffers by the billions of dollars' worth; in the postwar years, we were deeply concerned over the dollar shortage and applauded schemes like the Marshall Plan that were designed to overcome it. To find dollars a glut on world markets and our gold hoard shrunken by more than half was almost unthinkable; to watch Zurich gnomes, pompous generals, and cynical speculators look down their noses at the dollar was almost unbearable.

This is, I suppose, why most of what I have written on this subject has an unmistakable emotional bias. Every one of the pieces that follow takes the position that the dollar is fundamentally strong and that gold is a second-class commodity. We are going to have to shake the foundations of our monetary system a lot harder than they have been shaken already if I am to change my opinions on this subject.

Most important, however, my emotional bias has served me well: The position taken in these essays has indeed turned out to be correct. Despite all the panic-mongers and the weeping Willies and the cynics, the dollar is still the international currency of choice and the official price of gold remains rigidly set at $35 an ounce. Those people who invested in gold during the past 15 years or so have surely been badly served: Their asset has lost purchasing power, it has produced no income, and it has incurred carrying expenses besides.

Since international finance is apparently complicated for most people to understand, and since gold in particular stirs visceral emotional reactions among human beings, the myths and the received doctrines have a particularly strong appeal in this area. For this reason, too, the essays in this section are perhaps more strongly argued than those in the other parts of the book.

The general context in which most of the pieces were written should be clear enough, but one requires some special comment; namely, "The Threads of Gold from Schenectady to London," which I wrote for the November 1, 1960, issue of my investment-counsel firm's monthly bulletin.

At that time, financial people abroad became deeply concerned with the possible consequences if young John F. Kennedy were to become President of the United States. They read into his unfortunately casual campaign comments on the economic situation a strong bias toward inflation, indifference toward the international position of the dollar, and perhaps an inadequate respect for fixed exchange rates. As a result, they began buying gold at an accelerated pace in the London market; for the first time in history, gold was selling above $40 an ounce. This episode ultimately led to the formation of the famous London gold pool that was subsequently dissolved during a later crisis, in March 1968.

In any case, although I had been an investment counselor at that time for nearly 10 years and had been through some pretty scary episodes in the stock market, I had never seen my clients in such a state of panic. With the possible exception of the worst moments of the stock-market break of 1962, I must say that I have never seen them in such a state of panic since then, either. As I was convinced that the fundamentals of the situation were in much better shape than the excitement seemed to suggest, it was clear to me that this was clearly a moment when "the only thing we have to fear is fear itself." The real danger to the dollar was in the panic itself, not in the dollar's basic position. The objective, therefore, was to subdue the panic as soon as possible. The essay in question hit the real facts of the matter right on the button; in view of the atmosphere in which it was written and in view of the subsequent course of events

(Kennedy understood the balance-of-payments problem far better than the two Presidents who preceded him or followed him), this piece stands up remarkably well.

The first essay in this chapter, which precedes the one I have just described, was written for the *New York Times Magazine* in 1960 to describe the lore (and lure) of gold and to trace its history as a monetary standard; it ends up with a philosophical statement reflecting my skepticism about and distaste for the worshippers of gold. This viewpoint appears in stronger detail in an essay in the final chapter, "Is Gold the Only Thing That's Keeping Us Honest?"

The other pieces comprise a bit of amusing history, a basic explanation of the current international monetary system, a foray into the virtues of foreign trade, and a discussion of appropriate investment policies for a period of extreme international financial tension. The common thesis of all these essays is that, despite all the hue and cry, the dollar *is* still Number One.

GOLD IS STILL GOOD AS GOLD*

Gold is back in the headlines after 20 years of obscurity in the financial pages. Even though the outflow has recently been cut from a flood to a trickle, America's tremendous

---

* From the *New York Times Magazine*, May 15, 1960. Copyright © 1960 by The New York Times Company. Reprinted by permission.

gold hoard is still shrinking, as foreigners use some of their newly gained wealth to buy back from us a small portion of the gold they shipped here during the dark days before the war. We are selling them gold to settle our international accounts, for we have been paying more money to foreigners—for aid, investment, and imports—than they have been spending here.

Each time a foreign country purchases gold from us, an elaborate procedure is set in motion, beginning at Fort Knox. Here our national hoard is hidden away in a two-level granite, steel, and concrete vault. Behind a 20-ton airtight and watertight stainless-steel door, to which various members of the staff must dial a series of combinations, each of which is known to only one man, some 900,000 gold bricks are piled to the ceiling. In an area that combines the antiseptic character of a hospital with the severe impersonality of a prison ward is stacked more than $12 billion in wealth and immeasurable beauty (which casual visitors are not allowed to see).

When the order comes, the armed guards at Fort Knox haul out the gold and weigh it on scales so sensitive that even a pea would start them rocking. After all, at $35 an ounce, pea-sized quantities equal many dollars. Then the gold rises from the deep subterranean vaults into the daylight. But only briefly. After a trip whose security arrangements would satisfy the most nervous visiting potentate, the gold disappears again into the dungeons of the quasi-Florentine fortress of the Federal Reserve Bank in New York's financial district.

There it is weighed once more and carefully stacked in neat piles of bricks, to be held in the name of and at the disposal of the country that bought it from us. Usually it is left here in New York, in order to save the trouble and expense of shipping it across the ocean. However, many foreign bankers—and this includes the Russians—do frequently go down to the vaults of the Federal Reserve Bank to make sure that their country's gold is still there. (Here, other visitors are also allowed to have a look.)

Gold's role as the *sole* monetary standard of the world has been surprisingly brief. Although records of gold as a form of wealth go back to Egyptian times, 3,000 years before Christ, it was nevertheless too scarce throughout most of history to serve as the single standard of value. Iron and copper were used occasionally, but silver was gold's main competitor: It was more scarce than iron or copper and therefore more precious, but not so scarce as gold.

Thus, it was not until 1821 that Britain adopted gold as the single monetary standard for the pound sterling. And then another 50 years passed—after the tremendous discoveries of gold during the 1850s had been digested into the world's monetary systems—before France, Germany, and the United States joined the club. The rest of the world soon followed; by 1914, China and Mexico were the only important countries still using silver as their monetary base. Yet, by 1937, not one country continued to maintain a fixed tie between its currency and gold, and the arrangements in use today are only a faint shadow of the elaborate mechanism prevailing during gold's hegemony of 1880–1914.

But if the gold standard as we once knew it no longer exists (and many people believe that, by tying a nation's economy intimately and irretrievably to world economic trends, the gold standard involved a dangerous abdication of national economic independence), why does gold continue to serve so successfully as an international poker chip?

The answer is in the question itself. To paraphrase Gertrude Stein, gold is acceptable because it's acceptable because it's acceptable. Britain is glad to take gold from us, because she knows she can settle her payments balance with Germany in gold, and Germany will accept the gold from Britain because France or Holland or even the USSR. will accept it in payment of international obligations, and they in turn will accept it because . . .

Nevertheless, this lovely yellow metal has left a trail of pain and blood and death, which renders not a little grotesque our insistence on revering it not only as the source of all wealth, but also as a symbol of all that is beautiful and fine.

We respect the Golden Rule, dream of the Golden Age, delight at the Golden Wedding, reward a child who is good as gold. We call it a precious metal when it serves no use except adornment, while our civilization depends for its daily operation on far more precious metals, such as iron and copper and lead.

Freud ascribed our fascination with the yellow metal to the erotic fantasies and interests of earliest childhood: Gold is the sublimation of our infantile infatuation with dirt. Perhaps its extraordinary purity inspires men to violence and vileness.

While such unconscious motivations may be true, they depend upon a very matter-of-fact physical characteristic— gold is chemically inert and thus will not combine directly with oxygen. This means it retains its luster and does not tarnish; the magnificent gold jewelry of the ancients may be seen in the museums today shining as brilliantly as though it had been purchased at Cartier's only yesterday.

"If gold ruste," wrote Chaucer a long time ago, "what shall iren do?"

However, gold inspires passions deeper than the esthetic ones. The gold of the Coricancha, the Inca temple at Cuzco, along with thousands of other golden artworks created and worshiped by the Incas, was melted down by Pizarro and his men into ingots of standard size. Some they used for trade among themselves; a large part went back to Spain and formed the base of her eminence as a great power in the sixteenth and seventeenth centuries. The "civilized" Spaniards simply murdered any "primitive" Indians who objected.

Gold was discovered in California in January 1848, nine days before the sleepy Mexican colony was ceded to the United States. By 1850, 80,000 people had come to seek their fortune in the bear-infested hills, many traveling for months in incredible hardship and danger as their tiny Hudson River steamers made the long voyage through the Strait of Magellan.

A year later, Chinese, Australians, even Sandwich Islanders had joined with the Europeans and white and Indian Americans to swell the mining population alone to 140,000 men.

Today, one can recall the rugged life of the forty-niners by driving up U.S. Highway 49 near Mariposa, California, through towns named Mormon Bar, Quartzburg, Sutter Creek, Drytown, Gouge Eye, Mount Bullion. Here, amid the billboards and juke joints of our own day, is where the miners gambled away or drank up the few dollars most of them gained from panning in freezing streams and scraping their fingers to the bone in the craggy quartz.

Will Rogers, recalling his visit to the Klondike and Yukon, put it neatly when he observed: "There is a lot of difference in pioneering for gold and pioneering for spinach."

The most terrifying gold mining of all takes place in our own day in the mines of South Africa. Here the white man owns and profits from the gold but leaves to the black the ghastly business of digging it out.

The mines are deep in South Africa. Some go down as much as two miles. Thousands of miles of tunnels interlace this hell. The miners work in a nightmare atmosphere fouled by poisonous gases and quartz dust, amid the shattering clatter of great drills striking at the rocks.

When the day's work is over, they come back up to the earth's surface to try to sleep in their crowded compounds, carefully separated from their white employers, and a very long distance indeed from the neatly stacked gold bricks in the antiseptic vaults of Fort Knox.

As an instance of man's capacity to devour his fellow-man, the gold mines of Johannesburg have not even the rationalization that the metal goes to a good use. It just goes from one hole to another.

Are our desires for gold so sensible? John Ruskin once recalled the Midas legend when he told the story of a ship that was wrecked on the way home from California. "One of the passengers fastened a belt around him with two hundred pounds of gold in it, with which he was afterward found at the bottom. Now, as he was sinking, had he the gold? Or had the gold him?"

After Pearl Harbor, when the embattled Americans were making their last stand in the Philippines, a submarine crossed the Pacific on a vital mission. Was it sent to bring back some essential military equipment badly needed on another front, or perhaps to convey wounded boys to the safer sanctuary of Hawaii or San Francisco?

On the contrary, the cargo was even more "precious," for the gold stock of the Philippine government had to be protected from Japanese hands. Loaded with gold, the submarine dove below the surface of the sea and headed back eastward toward American shores. It arrived safely.

Perhaps we are finally reaching a time when a more rational view can prevail, when we can use less passionate stuff to serve the very important function of settling international payment balances. Premier Khrushchev observed not long ago: "Lenin said the day would come when gold would serve to coat the walls and floors of public toilets."

Another glimpse of the future was expressed—and more gracefully—by John Maynard Keynes:

> Gold no longer passes from hand to hand, and the touch of the metal has been taken away from men's greedy palms. The little household gods, who dwelt in purses and stockings and tin boxes, have been swallowed by a single golden image in each country, which lives underground and is not seen. Gold is out of sight—gone back into the soil.

Out of sight, out of mind? "When gods are no longer seen in a yellow panoply walking the earth, we begin to rationalize them," Keynes went on, "and it is not long before there is nothing left."

THE THREADS OF GOLD FROM SCHENECTADY TO LONDON*

It was indeed a cruel and strange stroke of fate that wild and frenzied speculation in gold occurred in the same

---

* A Bernstein-Macaulay bulletin, November 1, 1960.

week that the wage-price spiral in the United States was being buried. Can it be that the purchasing power of the dollar should have been questioned at the very moment that thousands of Westinghouse and General Electric employees were willing to abandon their cost-of-living escalation clauses and that radical West Coast longshoremen gave employers free rein in introducing labor-saving machinery?

What is the connection between the surrender of the International Union of Electrical Workers and the obsessive European speculators who paid $40 an ounce for gold? What has Harry Bridges' capitulation to do with the cold chill that swept through Wall Street in the week of October 17?

A great deal of argument, much of it superfluous, has been spent on the question of whether the postwar rise in prices caused the rise in wages or whether the rise in wages caused the rise in prices. But everyone agrees that there was an association between the two. Many people have argued that prices would stop going up if wage increases could be checked; others (including ourselves) predicted that wages would stop going up once businessmen found that they could no longer raise prices and get away with it.

The evidence clearly supports the contention that the wage-price spiral has been steadily slowing down and will slow down further. From 1945 to 1953, average hourly earnings in manufacturing rose at an annual rate of about

8 percent; from 1953 to 1959, the annual rate of increase was a little under 6 percent; in the past 12 months, average hourly earnings have risen less than 2 percent. In our bulletin one year ago, October 1, 1959, we wrote,

> The easy pattern of wage increases followed by more-than-offsetting price increases is being strangled to death in the current steel strike. . . . Meanwhile, the "war babies" will soon start to flood the labor market. The age group 20–64 grew by only 6.7 million people during the decade of the 1950s; in the next ten years, it will grow by more than 12 million. Within this environment, will wage rates increase by more than 50% as they did during the 1950s?

At the same time, discouraging and disappointing earnings reports for the first nine months of 1960 almost unanimously complain of price weaknesses and competitive pressures. They reflect concern over the inability of management to raise prices in the face of these conditions. Excess capacity is a problem that plagues most industries, not just a few. These trends show up in the consumer price index, which rose at an annual rate of around 16 percent from 1945 to 1953, then slowed down to less than 1 percent a year from 1953 to 1959, and today is actually below the level of 12 months ago.

In short, all of the fundamental trends in the economy have signaled the end of inflationary pressures in the

United States. Part of this is, of course, due to conservative monetary policies. But a good deal is the result of excess capacity, foreign competition, and rising average levels of unemployment. Union leaders are able to sense these factors all too clearly and to recognize that these more recent conditions are likely to prevail for the foreseeable future.

Thus, developments at General Electric, at Westinghouse, and in the West Coast shipping industry have been dramatic indications of the turn of events. It is a shame that they received so little attention in the press, because their significance is nothing short of tremendous. In fact, they are symptomatic of approaching problems of *de*flation, not *in*flation. No matter which candidate wins the popularity (or perhaps we should call it "least unpopularity") contest on November 8, expansionary or antirecessionary economic policies will only reduce the downward pressures on the price level; upward pressures in the prices of American goods and services are most unlikely. In short, it looks as though the dollar may soon buy more goods and services, not less.

In the light of all this, fear over the future purchasing power of the dollar appears ridiculous. Yet, as we have pointed out on other occasions, public attitudes toward gold, devaluation, and currency crises are packed with the most intense emotional dynamite. These reactions are extraordinarily difficult to control, once they get started. Nevertheless, while the value of the dollar and its gold backing do have some elements of uncertainty, while it would be foolish to insist that no problems exist, we continue to believe that the problems are soluble, that there is still room for maneuver and that only panic can topple the applecart.

The simple fact is that the United States is an incredibly rich and productive country. Anyone with eyes to see knows that. Furthermore, we hold nearly half the world's total monetary gold stock. Our gold reserve is larger by far relative to the goods and services we buy abroad than is the case with any other country. Billions of people in Asia, Africa, and Latin America are insatiably hungry for dollars to buy here the goods and services they so desperately need. For the full year 1960, our exports of goods and services (excluding transfers under military grants) will exceed our imports by at least $3 billion. Foreigners clearly find the dollar an attractive asset, as evidenced by a *rise* during the past 12 months of well over a billion dollars in their holdings of bank deposits and short-term securities in the United States.

Why, then, has the difficulty developed? The problem lies in our trade and military relations with Western Europe (especially Germany) and Japan, as compared with our relations with the rest of the world. In the 30 months ended June 30, 1960, for example, our commercial exports of goods and services to Western Europe and Japan exceeded our commercial imports from them by about $2 billion. But we spent almost $7 billion in these areas to maintain our troops and overseas military bases. Half of our private remittances went there. They also received almost \$2 billion, or around one-third, of our total long-term investments abroad. In short, we have been paying out to Western Europe and Japan substantial amounts of dollars in excess of what they have needed to buy goods and services from us. This is in sharp contrast with our relations with the countries of the rest of the world, where sales of our goods and services to them exceeded our imports from them by \$7 billion during this same 30-month period.

The wealthier nations of the world have more dollars than they need; the poorer ones have too few. Western Europe, Canada, and Japan hold nearly 70 percent of total short-term dollar assets—and their share is increasing. Thus, the plethora of dollars in certain areas leads to the suggestion that the dollar has become a "soft currency," when it is a hard currency indeed to billions of people in the hungry areas of the world.

From this unbalanced situation stems the insistence that our Western European and Japanese friends must contribute a larger share of the military costs and the aid to underdeveloped countries that the pursuit of the cold war demands. Some downward revision in their interest rates would also be most salutary. Without these steps, America will have to protect the dollar by import quotas, tariffs, exchange controls, and even withdrawal of troops and equipment from bases abroad. These are hardly attractive alternatives, but they should be used as bargaining counters to bring the wealthier countries of the world into line.

And let the impetuous European speculators listen to the complaints of American union members about the slow rate of wage increases. Let them note the widespread concern here over price weakness in nearly every industry. Let them heed the urgent need for dollars in the poor and hungry areas of the world. Let them remember the rapidly rising wage levels in Western Europe and Japan. And then, in calmness, not in panic, let them tell us whether the dollar is really such a weak currency, losing its purchasing power, a drug on world markets. Where are the real bargains developing in the world? The facts are most reassuring.

À LA RECHERCHE DU TEMPS PASSÉ*

The recent Soviet bid to buy American wheat stirs memories of a similar sequence of events 72 years ago. In 1891, crop failures in Europe and an abundant harvest in the United States combined to rescue us from a balance-of-payments crisis even more intense than the one we are now experiencing. These events of 1891 are worth recalling, for they provide an interesting and significant perspective to the difficulties we face today.

---

* A Bernstein-Macaulay bulletin, November 1, 1963.

In the latter part of the 1880s, the United States Treasury Department was engaged in an operation that most of us today would find most curious, to say the least. It was doing its best to get out from under an accumulated budget surplus that was actually embarrassing! A sequence of years in which budget receipts had been swollen by a combination of high tariff rates and large commercial imports had concentrated an excessive amount of money in the vaults of the Treasury. This apparently disturbing situation had led Congress to introduce the quaint institution now known as "pork barrel legislation"—taking the form of large and frequently wasteful public-works expenditures. Repayment of the public debt at high premiums for repurchased bonds was also progressing at a rapid pace.

As a result of both of these policies, the Treasury was paying out considerably more money than it was taking in. The impact on the economy, as it usually is under such conditions, was highly expansionary. Money in circulation increased and trade expanded rapidly. Prices rose, imports burgeoned, exports shrank. To complicate matters, Baring Brothers, a major London banking house, nearly failed as a consequence of economic disasters and a bloody revolution in Argentina: This pricking of London's foreign-investment bubble led to wholesale liquidation of foreign securities by the British, including substantial withdrawals from New York.

A massive outflow of gold from the United States got under way. In fact, we lost more gold in the first six months of 1891 than we had lost in any 12-month period since the Civil War. Fear spread, as it has in recent years, that the U.S. gold stock would fall so low that dollars would no longer be redeemable into gold on demand. Polite rationalizations and obfuscations by politicians did little to help the situation. The Secretary of the Treasury even went so far as to try to ascribe the gold outflow to expenditures by American tourists at the highly popular Paris World's Fair.

At the crucial moment, a most miraculous accident of nature occurred. While the European wheat crops of both 1889 and 1890 had been small and had forced substantial drafts on existing stockpiles, the crop of 1891 was a complete failure in Europe's major breadbaskets—Russia and France. Meanwhile, on this side of the ocean, the United States produced the largest wheat crop up to that point in its history. Europe's wheat production in 1891 was 156 million bushels below 1889; our own crop rose by 255 million bushels and exceeded by fully 100 million bushels the largest crop then on record.

Of course, the impact on our balance of payments was dramatic. Our merchandise exports for the 12 months ended June 30, 1892, exceeded $1 billion for the first time in our history and were $150 million above the preceding 12 months, all of this increase resulting from larger exports of foodstuffs. Meanwhile, our imports were declining. As a result, our export surplus swelled emphatically from $40 million to more than $200 million—a figure exceeded only three times before that year. Gold poured back into our coffers. For the moment at least, nature had saved the day.

Now once again our balance-of-payments difficulties are going to be alleviated by an accident of nature. As in 1957, when the Suez Canal was out of commission, the abundant raw-material resources of the New World will come to the rescue of the Old.

The recent sequence of events is a dramatic reminder of the overwhelming importance and urgency of food supplies. No economy, no matter whether it is capitalist or socialist or whatever, can progress and develop until it can feed its urban population as well as its farmers and peasants. Industrial development must wait upon the assurance of an efficient agricultural economy to feed adequately all the workers who move from the land to the factory, to construction, and to the office. The English taught the rest of the world an unforgettable lesson in the 1840s, relevant to this very day, when they solved this problem by dropping all tariffs on imports of grain, thus enabling them to buy their food cheaply abroad and to concentrate their efforts in industry, where their natural resources and capabilities far excelled the rest of the world at that time.

But, perhaps more important, the experiences of 1891 and 1963 put a dramatic perspective on the fabulous productivity of American agriculture. How ironic it is that we devote so much time and effort to throttling down the most extraordinarily fertile and efficient sector of our economy!

It is ironic, in part, because millions of people throughout the world are close to starvation. But it is also a symptom of the Humpty-Dumpty economics by which we live. In elementary economics courses we learn the Law of Comparative Advantage—that countries will export those goods and services in which their productive efficiency is furthest ahead of everybody else in the world—and surely American agriculture has a comparative advantage over all other food producers. Yet, we go to incredibly elaborate and sophisticated lengths to repress our food production and to keep our prices above the levels that the poorer countries of the world can afford to pay.

This is not our fault alone. Vested interests in agriculture are stubborn and shortsighted throughout the world, as the recent chicken controversy with the Common Market so clearly illustrates. Yet, somehow it makes little sense. The unabashed Soviet admiration for the farmers of Iowa, the world's pressing demand for America's food supplies, and the truly miraculous productivity of our farms make a mockery of the artificial and archaic financial and legislative arrangements by which we choose to live.

History teaches us that bondage of this type ultimately breaks asunder. As in 1891, recent events are an encouraging reminder of America's fundamental economic strength.

DEVALUATION, DEFICITS, AND DELUSIONS*

For reasons that surely need no elaboration here, money is an emotion-packed subject. Few of us have a really rational attitude toward it, and all of us are captives of myths and shibboleths about it that we have inherited from a largely irrelevant past. Yet, the study of money is much less intricate than it seems. The trouble is that we have such difficulty in approaching it objectively.

This is certainly the case with the issues and problems that face us today. Devaluation of the dollar has been an active topic of conversation for several years. In addition, we are now moving into a period when the federal government's revenues are going to fall well short of expenditures. Does this mean that we must have inflation? And does it mean that we must devalue the dollar? This bulletin is an effort to explain in simple terms what is involved in the answers to these questions.

Technically, devaluation involves a change in the relationship between a nation's monetary unit, on the one hand, and gold, on the other. If, for example, the U.S. Treasury changes its buying and selling price for gold from its current rate of $35 an ounce to $45 (or by just about 30 percent), each dollar would then be equal to only 1/45th of an ounce of gold instead of 1/35th of an ounce; the dollar would be

---

* A Bernstein-Macaulay bulletin, August 1, 1962.

worth less in terms of gold and, in that sense, would be "devalued." Although the appearances differ, this is really the same as what happened in olden times when the value of coins was determined by the quantity of precious metals they contained—the monarch then "debased" the currency by using less precious metal in the coins while he continued to print the same value on them.

If other countries made no change in the relationship between their currencies and gold, the dollar would be devalued in terms of these other currencies as well. Today, an ounce of gold can be purchased in the United States for $35 an ounce and shipped to England, where it will fetch £12 10s.; if the dollar is devalued to $45 an ounce, however, $35 will then buy less than an ounce of gold and will bring only a little over £9 7s. in English money. This also means that English goods will seem more expensive to us, as we would then have to pay $45 for £12 10s. of English merchandise. An Englishman, on the other hand, would be able to buy $35 worth of merchandise here for only £9 7s. instead of £12 10s. Thus, our exports would rise and our imports would fall.

But while devaluation does have an effect on our international financial transactions, it need make little difference to us domestically. The man with $1,000 in the bank would still have $1,000 there, regardless of what happened to the price of gold.

Nevertheless, many people believe that devaluation means not only that the dollar would lose purchasing power abroad but that, in addition, it would lead prices to rise at home so that the dollar would buy less here as well. Is this conclusion valid?

The point is that devaluation creates certain conditions that *can* lead to price inflation, but that is quite different from saying that these conditions *will* lead to price inflation:

- By automatically raising the dollar value of the nation's gold stock by 30 percent, the Treasury would have created out of thin air five billion additional dollars that it could theoretically spend without having to tax anybody, or to issue any new debt.

- As this money is paid out to individuals and corporations, it would end up as new deposits in the banking system. This would increase the money available to the banks for lending and investing and would thus form the base for an additional wave of new credit creation. Surely, then, an inflationary potential would have been established.

- But while this is a necessary, it is by no means a sufficient condition for inflation. *If the Treasury never spent the gold profit, nothing would happen.* The 1933 gold profit, for example, was never used to finance normal governmental programs that, under our system of government, are expected to clear the appropriation process established by the Constitution and by Congressional usage.

The most casual student of American history or the American political system would find no basis for believing that any administration or Congress we would elect would be so irresponsible as to pour this money into the economy on a wholesale scale. Our expenditures are in any case limited by Congressional appropriations, so that no administration would be able to spend the gold profit simply because it is there. Furthermore, the Federal Reserve has ample powers to offset any increase in the money supply that might result. The direct domestic inflationary impact of a devaluation is therefore likely to be negligible.

But why do countries devalue, anyway? Two sets of forces lead countries to devalue their currencies—one fundamental, the other psychological:

1. In the long run, the value of a nation's currency in the foreign-exchange markets is determined by the relationship between its imports and its exports and by the inflow and outflow of long-term capital investments. As devaluation is, in effect, an across-the-board reduction in the prices that foreigners have to pay for American products and an across-the-board increase that we would have to pay for things purchased abroad, devaluation tends to increase exports and to attract foreign long-term capital, on the one hand, and to discourage imports and to reduce the outflow of long-term capital, on the other hand. Thus, devaluation

restores balance to international financial relationships that are overburdened by an excess of payments to foreigners and a shortage of receipts from them.

2. But devaluation may be unavoidable even if the fundamental trends of a country's balance of international payments are improving. The mere suspicion that devaluation may be in the wind or that people may be prevented from freely converting their holdings of a given currency into the currency of other countries may cause a wholesale flight of capital. When such a "run on the bank" occurs, the authorities may have no choice but to suspend gold payments and then to devalue.

The United States at the present time is faced with an improvement in its fundamental position but a deterioration in the psychological influences on its currency.

As we pointed out as long ago as our bulletins of September and November 1960, the true purchasing power and international position of the dollar has in fact been improving. Prices in the United States today are stable or—as any businessman will regretfully testify—tending to move downward. The upward sweep of wage rates here is slowing down significantly. Military expenditures abroad are being cut while foreigners are buying more military equipment here. Foreign-aid outlays are increasingly tied to the purchase of American goods, Meanwhile, prices and wages in the major industrial countries that are our main competitors (and our best customers, too) are rising much faster than they are here. Finally, the Treasury and the Federal Reserve have together taken a variety of steps to bulwark the defenses around the dollar. Perhaps most important, we can draw on the enormous resources of the International Monetary Fund to supplement our own reserves of gold and foreign exchange.

Despite the accumulation of these trends that are favorable to us, nervousness about the future of the dollar persists and is even increasing. Even though our position is improving and will probably improve still more rapidly in the future, the excess of payments to foreigners during the recent past has cut our gold stock by $6 billion since 1957 while our short-term liabilities to foreigners have risen by $8 billion during the same period. We now have $16 billion in gold, while foreigners have demand claims on us to the tune of $23 billion. This has naturally led to uncertainty and anxiety, because clearly we will be unable to meet our obligations if everybody wants gold at the same moment.

But the same is true of the soundest bank. No banker can pay off all of his depositors if they all want to withdraw all their deposits at the same moment. With our gold equal to 70 percent of our short-term liabilities, our own position is actually far more comfortable than the British position ever was when they were bankers to the world—they have always felt things were under control when their liabilities ran as high as three times the size of their gold and foreign-exchange reserves.

What this means—in the most literal sense of the words—is that we have nothing to fear but fear itself. There is little or no economic justification for devaluation of the dollar. The only real danger comes from the *fear* of devaluation, which can lead to speculative withdrawals from the United States—a "run on the bank," in other words—that will give us no choice but to suspend gold payments and ultimately to devalue. In the light of all this, a thorough understanding of exactly what is going on is crucially important for the protection of the dollar itself.

Nevertheless, at first glance, devaluation looks like a wonderful solution to our problems. With the stroke of a pen, we will write up our gold stock so that it is at least equal to if not worth even more than our liabilities to foreigners. Our exports will rise, while our imports will shrink. This will stimulate business activity here and restore equilibrium to our balance of international payments. Speculative movements against the dollar will cease. On the assumption that, no matter which party is in Washington, we shall have responsible government, the inflationary potentials of devaluation will be avoided. Why, then, is devaluation looked upon as an undesirable move?

- On the political side, we have an obligation of good faith to those countries that have been willing to hold dollars in large sums rather than converting their dollars into gold or other currencies. This refers in particular to our staunchest allies—the Western

Europeans and the Japanese. If we were to devalue, these countries would sustain an enormous loss.

- This is hardly the way to keep friends and influence people. Any businessman who breaks his word has an almost impossible time rebuilding his business in the long run, no matter how much advantage he may gain in the short run. After the British devalued in 1931, it took many years before confidence in Britain's word and currency was restored. Indeed, much of the fetish for gold in today's relatively sophisticated financial world can be traced to the continued reverberation, even after more than 30 years, of the shock waves of the devaluation of sterling in 1931.

- Since, therefore, we would be unable to pull off a devaluation as a surprise to our friends, we would have to do it in consultation with them. And their assent would be most unlikely. Their foreign-trade position would be seriously damaged, while they would be incurring losses on their dollar investments here. Therefore, either they would agree to a devaluation of the dollar so small as to be meaningless, or they would devalue right along with us. This would leave things little better than they are today: The only real gainers would be the gold miners, which means that it would be a real bonanza for the Russians.

But what will happen if the budget is in deficit? Many people believe that a country running a large budget deficit must ultimately devalue its currency. And if enough people believe this, even though it is by no means necessarily the truth, a budget deficit will in fact lead to a flight from the dollar and to devaluation. An understanding of the realities is, therefore, extremely important.

In the "old days"—that is, before 1933—almost every country's currency was freely convertible into gold by *all* holders. From the late 1870s to 1933, for example, anyone in the United States could exchange paper currency or bank deposits for gold on demand. But this also meant that, as the money supply of a country increased, the claims on that country's gold stock were also increasing. Therefore, a budget deficit that led to an increase in the money supply frequently led in turn to doubts that free convertibility into gold could be maintained, the doubts then led to a rush to convert into gold, and the "run on the bank" led inevitably to suspension of gold payments and then to devaluation. From this sequence of events the belief grew—and still persists—that budget deficits must lead to devaluation.

But the situation today is entirely different. We allow free conversion of dollars into gold only to foreign governments and central banks, so that it is their holdings *and only their holdings* of dollars relative to our gold stock that are really relevant. If a tax cut in the United States leads to a budget deficit and Americans hold more dollars as a result, that has no relation to the foreign-exchange value of the dollar. And if, at the same time, it fosters economic growth, leads to modernization of our plant and equipment, and enhances the attractions to foreigners for investing in the United States, a tax cut may actually tend to improve our balance of payments. If the balance of payments improves, the chances of devaluation are lessened rather than increased. *This sequence of events has been precisely the experience of those European countries that we think of as having the hardest currencies in the world today.*

Of course, if a budget deficit leads to price inflation here, our balance of payments may deteriorate. But price inflation is far from an inevitable result of a budget deficit. The primary trend of commodity prices today is downward: A budget deficit *may* prevent prices from falling further, but, with the uncomfortably large surplus of labor and productive capacity with which we are now burdened, a major and sustained rise in the American price level is most unlikely. It will be even more unlikely if, as seems probable, an expansionary budgetary policy is accompanied by a relatively conservative monetary policy.

The reflex action that associates budget deficits with devaluation relates to the days when power-hungry monarchs financed personal wars by debasing the currency and to the days when the local money supply was directly tied to the gold stock. Furthermore, given our primitive and somewhat romantic fascination with gold, devaluation of the dollar in terms of gold admittedly has the elements of a powerful emotional shock: Fear, even if irrational, is still understandable.

But it would be a cruel twist of fate indeed if the dollar had to be devalued at a time when our balance of payments is fundamentally improving, when inflation at home has finally been conquered, and when an excessively delayed reform of our fiscal policies is finally being accepted by both political parties. An improvement in our economic strength is hardly the moment for the dollar to be held in doubt. If, then, we are ultimately forced to devalue, it will come about only because of the panic of the ignorant and the malevolence of the fear-mongers.

THE COMMON MARKET: CHALLENGE OR SALVATION?*

One hundred and twenty years ago, Frederic Bastiat, a brilliant French economist and satirist, composed the following "petition" to the Chamber of Deputies:

> PETITION OF THE MANUFACTURERS OF
> CANDLE-STICKS, WAX-LIGHTS, LAMPS . . .
> AND GENERALLY EVERYTHING
> CONNECTED WITH LIGHTING:

> We are suffering from the intolerable competition of a foreign rival, placed, so it would seem, in a condition so far superior to our own for the production of light, that he absolutely inundates

---

* A Bernstein-Macaulay bulletin, January 2, 1962.

our national market with it at a price fabulously reduced. . . . This rival . . . is no other than the sun.

What we pray for is that it may please you to pass a law ordering the shutting up of all windows, skylights, etc.—in a word, all openings, holes, chinks, and fissures. . . .

If you shut up as much as possible all access to natural light and create a demand for artificial light, which of our French manufacturers will not benefit by it?

Make your choice, but be logical; for as long as you exclude, as you do, iron, corn, foreign fabrics, in proportion as their prices approximate to zero, what inconsistency it would be to admit the light of the sun, the price of which is already at zero during the entire day!

In these days, when tariffs and international trade are once again front-page news, Bastiat's acid barbs against protectionism are appropriate indeed. They give meaning and perspective to the flow of verbiage that has gushed out in recent weeks.

The vitally important truth of which Bastiat reminds us is that the more cheaply we can buy abroad, the more money we will have to spend at home. This is the crucial point in the whole matter: Anything that interferes with trade causes a corresponding drop in living standards. What we are seldom told, and what we must never forget, is that

Americans as consumers can improve their living standards if goods are made available to them at lower prices—don't we gain if we can buy our clothes or our cameras or our toys or our typewriters more cheaply? If we are prevented from buying our goods and services at the lowest possible prices, then each of us will have to work harder and have to earn more in order to sustain the same standard of living.

This means that the injury caused to some industries by low-cost imports is offset by the gain to everybody else in being able to buy at lower prices. And if we can buy a given quantity of goods and services for less money by purchasing them abroad, it follows that we shall have more money available to spend on other things at home. If we spend less on cameras, for example, we can afford to spend more on film.

Bastiat's petition from the candlestick makers puts the issue neatly. If we had to pay for our daylight, we would create jobs for candlestick makers, but we would have less to spend on other things—this is hardly a method for improving living standards. So long as sunlight is freely admitted to the earth, we can enjoy the pleasures and utility of daylight and still have money left over to spend on other goods and services.

This means, in short, that we are correct in fostering international trade to the greatest possible degree: It serves so well to raise real incomes and living standards. Of course, like other forms of economic progress, it leaves some localized injury in its wake. But then our objective must be not to block progress, but to ease the adjustments it necessitates. This is precisely the tack that the present Administration is taking.

The focus of attention in these matters is now toward the emerging Common Market in Western Europe. There is widespread fear that American exports will be unable to compete in our most important market, while other American industries will be hurt by a rising flood of low-cost imports. Both of these dangers exist, but they obscure the overriding consideration that we as consumers will have higher living standards, as will our European friends as well, if we can do our buying in the tempting market that growing efficiency and relatively low labor costs will make possible in Western Europe.

Furthermore, while American exporters may find that Europeans will be able to undersell them in some types of goods and services, we must make certain that at least we can avoid having to overcome discriminatory tariff walls in addition. The Common Market governments will not drop their discriminatory external tariff wall just to be nice: They will do it only if we are willing simultaneously to admit their goods and services to our own shores on a less restrictive basis. If we resort instead to higher tariffs and import quotas, we will gain nothing, for all of us will have to pay more for the things we buy, and foreign discrimination against our products will hurt output and employment in our export industries at the same time.

167

Some observers believe that we are up against a hopeless battle. They argue we will lose out because of our high and rising labor costs, the shortsighted attitudes of our union leaders, the many rigidities and restrictions of our administered price structure and oligopolistic markets, and the inflationary policies of our government. They expect that we will simply be unable to compete against the increasing economies of large-scale production as the Common Market countries drop their tariff barriers vis-à-vis one another and as they enjoy the benefits of relatively low labor costs.

But the pessimists have lost sight of the stimulus that trade and competition give to a progressive and dynamic economy—they have lost their faith in free enterprise, in competition, in Adam Smith. And the record speaks against them. The dramatic revival of the cartelized, antiquated and creaking French economy in recent years is proof enough of how invigorating the sharp-tasting medicine of competition can be. On our own shores, we can see this in the way the automobile industry stifled the threat of foreign imports in the past two years, in the heavy flow of capital spending on more efficient equipment by the steel industry in 1960–1961 when output was at low levels, in rising foreign sales of textiles and clothing by enterprising American manufacturers, in the persistently vigorous demand for American machinery of all types, in the dominance of American aircraft on the world's commercial airlines, and in the export of American coal to Newcastle and the Ruhr. The chairman of Bell and Howell recently expressed pride in the manner in which a 40 percent cut in camera tariffs "brought out the best of creativity in our industry."

On the other hand, limiting trade, reducing competition, supporting high prices negate the very tenets of capitalism and the American way; they protect special privileges, shelter the inefficient, and stifle initiative. As President Kennedy recently commented, those who are unwilling to adjust to competition *must* lose out in the long run, "for in order to avoid exertion, they accept paralysis."

We see nothing in the history of American industry to suggest that we will be unable to meet this test. On the contrary, our only real danger is in our reluctance to stand up to it.

IS THE DOLLAR STILL NUMBER ONE?*

Those of us who work in the financial community these days are so continuously bombarded with predictions of disaster that we become numb to most of them and skeptical about the rest. Our clients and friends, however, who for better or for worse are further removed from the daily turmoil of the security markets, hear just enough horror

---

* A Bernstein-Macaulay bulletin, June 1, 1968.

stories to bring them close to a state of panic but still hear too little to be able to laugh these stories off.

Thus, we are asked with increasing frequency whether people should put all their money into Swiss francs or into gold stocks or into Treasury bills to protect themselves against The Worst. Will devaluation of the dollar open the floodgates to uncontrolled inflation in which only the most occult forms of inflation hedges will be safe havens for accumulated wealth? Our answer to these questions is—No, you should not take these steps. The purpose of this bulletin is to explain why the investor should pursue an investment program more or less the same as the program he would pursue if matters had never come to the critical point at which they now stand.

We stress that our purpose here is neither to consider the likelihood of a devaluation of the dollar nor to argue its pros and cons. We are simply trying to assess its investment consequences if it does occur.

Of course, a devaluation of the dollar could take one of two forms. The first and most likely would be a devaluation in terms of gold, as a result of which we would declare our willingness to sell and buy gold at some price higher than $35, but at the same time the exchange rate between the dollar and sterling, francs, marks, guilders, and so on would remain substantially unchanged. A second but less likely form would involve both an increase in the official price of gold and a change in the relationship between the dollar and other currencies; in this event, one dollar would buy, say, only four francs instead of five, three marks instead of four, 500 lire instead of 600, and so on.

The first and probably the most important consideration is that no one has a very clear idea—and no one is even able to predict—what the chain of events would be like between now and the moment of devaluation. A vigorous effort to defend the dollar would involve strong deflationary medicine probably combined with more direct controls. This would be bearish for golds, bullish for bonds, and would reduce the attraction of sending money abroad. It would all depend on how irresistible are the pressures working toward devaluation, and the pressures against it still have considerable force. When the event finally did occur, American common stocks would probably work out much better than golds or foreign investments.

A second important fact to keep in mind is that a devaluation of the dollar in terms of gold alone would have almost no unfavorable *internal economic* impact on the United States. It would damage those nations that have been our friends and held dollars instead of gold. It would open up a credibility gap of enormous and dangerous proportions. It might lead to more speculative hoarding of gold by those who would then be convinced that its price had no upper limit. It might create some uncertainty in international trade and investment. However, dollars would continue to buy as many American goods and services as they would have bought anyway; any inflationary consequences that could follow upon an increase in the price of gold can be neutralized completely by Federal Reserve action. There would certainly be no advantage in holding foreign currencies instead of dollars under these circumstances.

A devaluation of the dollar in terms of other currencies might result in a profit to the investor who sent his capital outside the United States in anticipation of this event. But no one knows how long he would have to wait or whether the profit would be large enough to justify the risks involved.

And the risks are real: It is impossible to conceive of an event of this nature taking place except under utterly chaotic conditions in the foreign-exchange markets. Furthermore, since the proportion of gross national product accounted for by foreign trade and investment in other countries is far greater than it is here, the consequences to them would be much more serious. The collapse of the international financial system will, in fact, lead to a drastic decline in international trade and finance because of the enormous uncertainties and the direct controls that would inevitably follow upon it. Under these conditions, as in the 1930s, the greater relative strength of the American economy would be fully apparent; dollars would seem most attractive as a haven for capital.

Ultimately internal forces rather than foreign exchange and gold do determine the real strength of a currency. A month ago, the French franc looked very strong indeed.

Yet, had General de Gaulle been less interested in hoarding gold and more interested in the welfare of the French working classes, inflationary as that might have been, the French would have less gold today but the franc would look a lot stronger. The Midas legend never loses its significance.

In short, sending money abroad seems to make little sense. Unless the dollar were to be devalued in terms of other currencies, there would be no advantage at all; if unilateral devaluation did occur, conditions abroad would be so disturbed that no one would want to hold foreign currencies and the American investor might be unable to repatriate his money just when he would be most eager to do so.

A modest hedge in gold stocks might still be attractive to some people. But the sequence of events discussed here is by no means a sure thing, nor is gold any longer a commodity with an officially determined floor to its price. Hence, we would strongly oppose any wholesale conversion of holdings from good American companies to shares in gold mines. On the contrary, we continue to believe that the best investment choices remain among those companies that can survive and prosper regardless of the ultimate outcome of the present financial turmoil.

Chapter 5

HOW WRONG CAN YOU BE?

Prediction at best is a hazardous activity, but sometimes you can be so wrong that the only value in the results is the hilarity they provide.

In 1959, I was retained by the New York Stock Exchange to prepare projections of share volume over the next 20 years. On the strength of that assignment (which worked out well—nothing that has happened since has been outside the range of possibilities I suggested at that time), the American Stock Exchange asked me in 1962 to prepare a similar set of projections for them.

This was a tricky job. The character of the American Exchange was entirely different from that of the Big Board. In addition, the Etherington regime had just taken over from an inept management that had left the Exchange's reputation severely damaged. Hence, the future of this particular market for stocks was unusually difficult to predict.

The short piece that follows is a direct quote from the highlights of the findings in the published version of my work. It is followed by a brief description of what actually happened to volume on the American Stock Exchange during the decade of the 1960s.

I was well paid for my labors; when you compare the projections with the actual figures, you might argue that I was substantially overpaid.

THE AMERICAN STOCK EXCHANGE: PROSPECTS FOR FUTURE GROWTH

The trends of American Stock Exchange activity in the past suggest the following three prospects for the future:

1. Under relatively stable conditions and given a period of normal growth as evidenced in the 1950s, daily average volume by 1970 should reach 2.2 to 2.5 million shares, up approximately 25 percent from the record year 1961, when volume averaged two million shares a day. As long as a sustained bear market is avoided, the possibilities are excellent that average daily volume by 1970 will not drop below the two million mark. This would be about 60 percent greater than the 1962 level.

2. Even under the most pessimistic assumptions of a continuing recession through the 1960s, the daily average volume of trading on the American Stock Exchange by 1970 should range from 1.1 million to

1.4 million shares. This is 22 percent to 55 percent greater than the relatively active years 1955–1957.

3. In a sustained bull market, daily average volume could rise to about 3.6 million shares with a level of 4.4 million a day over extended periods. This would be almost double the record level of 1961, quadruple the 1955–1957 average, and 10 times the volume that prevailed in the early years after World War II. There may be days when trading on the exchange exceeds six million shares.

The middle-ground projection cited above—with relatively stable business conditions, normal economic growth, and a daily level of trading of 2.2 to 2.5 million shares—is considered by the Exchange staff as the proper level on which to base future planning.

The number of shares listed on the Exchange by the end of the decade is expected to range between 2.6 billion and 4.1 billion, with a stock list totaling 3.3 billion shares, 83 percent higher than at present, considered the most likely level.

What Happened Afterward:

Year	Average Daily Volume (millions)	High Day (millions)	Shares Listed (billions)
1963	1.3	2.8	1.7
1964	1.5	2.9	1.8
1965	2.1	5.0	1.7

Year	Average Daily Volume (millions)	High Day (millions)	Shares Listed (billions)
1966	2.7	6.6	1.8
1967	4.5	8.3	1.9
1968	6.4	10.1	2.2
1969	4.9	11.3	2.6

As the table shows, we were not only way off base—we were nowhere in the neighborhood of the ball park. The "proper level on which to base future planning" for 1970, or 2.2 to 2.5 million shares a day, was surpassed in 1966; the projected daily average for a "sustained bull market" at the end of the decade, or about four million shares a day, was exceeded in 1967. The suggested possibility of a high day in excess of six million shares after 1970 was actually reached four years ahead of time, in 1966. Volume in 1968 clearly broke through all of the parameters of the study.

The fantastic underestimation of volume during the second half of the decade would have been excusable in some degree if the number of shares listed on the American Exchange had turned out to be much larger than the number we had anticipated, for obviously the number of shares traded will bear some relationship to the number of shares listed. However, the actual figure for the number of shares listed was still only 2.4 billion in mid-1969, still below our *minimum* expectation of 2.6 billion shares for 1970 and nowhere near our "most likely" level of 3.3 billion.

It was, in fact, the turnover rates that fooled us completely, as more and more large investors began speculating in Amex stocks. The percentage of listed shares that changed hands each year had ranged from a low of 11 percent to a high of 27 percent between 1947 and 1961; between 1954 and 1961, turnover rates held between a range of 17 percent to 27 percent. We had projected our low estimate on an assumption of 13 percent turnover, our high estimate on 22 percent, and our "normal" estimate on 17 percent turnover a year. Here are the actual figures for annual turnover rates during the 1960s:

Year	Annual Volume as Percent of Listed Shares
1961	27.2
1962	17.1
1963	18.2
1964	21.2
1965	30.9
1966	37.8
1967	61.4
1968	72.5
1969	47.1

How wrong can you be?

Chapter 6

THE ECONOMIST AS PORTFOLIO MANAGER

T hese essays set forth the basic philosophical approach that I bring to the profession of portfolio management.

I use the word *profession* advisedly and with due care. Portfolio management must put the client's interest above that of the manager's and must therefore be carried on in such a way that conflicts of interest are kept to an absolute minimum. I say this because, in nearly every case, the funds placed in the care of the portfolio manager represent somebody's life savings or hard-earned accumulations; they are to protect and enhance the happiness and safety of the people who are dependent upon them. The manager of even the most impersonal type of institutional portfolio must always remember that there are human beings who will benefit or suffer from his decisions.

For this reason, in planning portfolio strategies, I have always been obsessed—perhaps too much so in some instances—with a rather negative but overwhelmingly important question: *What are the consequences if I am wrong?* I should stress that this question need by no means lead to an excessively conservative investment philosophy, for it has led me on a number of occasions to take much bigger risks for a client than a more conventional approach would have suggested as appropriate. But I do believe that no investment decisions can be rationally arrived at unless they are a logical part of a strategy based upon the answer to this question.

This question really relates to the whole problem of risk, which is an inescapable component of the investment process. We simply do not know what the future holds. This means that we are perforce going to be wrong a certain amount of the time—but we also never know which decision it is that will be the incorrect one (we are often right, in fact, for reasons that we never anticipated: is this actually being right or being wrong?). Hence, we must move ahead always on the assumption that the next decision may be the wrong one and with the realization that we must face the consequences if it is.

The consequences of being wrong essentially involve an examination of the opportunities to recoup any losses that may be incurred. And these opportunities will be determined by two different sets of conditions.

The first and most important condition is staying power. An investor who has a substantial income or a significant amount of cash reserves that can sustain him regardless of what happens to his securities can let time work in his favor in recouping losses; the greatest disasters are really limited only to those investors who are forced to liquidate at moments dictated by external events—a loan to be repaid, a job lost, a tax bill not reserved for—rather than at moments dictated by investment considerations only.

Staying-power considerations can also raise very complicated questions in planning portfolio strategy. The client who lives beyond his income and therefore draws down his capital each year needs capital gains in order to replenish his dwindling assets; on the other hand, the continuous invasion of his principal means that liquidation is being dictated by external events and that his staying power is limited. Here you need to take large risks but can ill afford to do so. The client whose income exceeds outgo (such as many institutional portfolios) obviously has no liquidation problems for a long time to come and can therefore afford to take large risks in the search for capital gains; on the other hand, the continuous additions to the client's assets mean that his capital is growing without having incurred any risks. Here you can afford to take the risks but do not need to.

The second condition for recouping losses is the nature of the investor's decision-making ability. Given a reasonable period of time, because markets do fluctuate, it takes an extraordinary series of poor judgments to do a really bad job of investing. You may fail to make a killing or even to run with the fastest of the crowd, but it is really difficult to lose money at investing if you have the staying power to carry you over the bleak periods.

I make this rather bald statement on the basis of an important fact of arithmetic: You can lose no more than 100 percent of the money you invest in any one security, but you can make an infinite amount on it. This apparently obvious and superficial statement tells us something that is overwhelmingly significant for investors: A few good guesses can far outweigh many poor ones. If you put $10,000 into each of five stocks, and if you lost 50 percent on four of them (which is a pretty terrible batting average), you can come out ahead overall if the fifth more than triples.

Thus, the consequences of the inevitable wrong decisions can be kept to a minimum if the investor has the staying power to remain in the game until the next throw of the dice and to avoid involuntary liquidation at the wrong moment. But the consequences can also be minimized if the investor has the time and opportunity to make a few lucky decisions that can readily offset the less fortunate ones.

The greater the staying power, the greater the risks the investor can take to try to find that magic killing.

Consequently, I would rather take large risks with a small proportion of the investor's money than to take a lot of small risks with most of his money. By the same token, I would rather have significant positions in five to ten securities than smaller positions in 15 or 20.

The first essay that follows has to do with the philosophy of pension-fund investing, but it will be as relevant to an individual investor as to an institutional one, because it illustrates a practical application of the philosophy I have expressed here. Since I believe strongly in aggressive rather than defensive investing, my approach is always to secure conditions that will make aggressive investing possible; the technique suggested to the pension-fund managers is to be so well protected against the consequences of being wrong that they can really step out with the aggressive part of the portfolios.

On the other hand, "Have You Met Mr. Jones?" should interest institutional managers, even though it tells the story of an individual investor. Mr. Jones, who was someone who actually came to my office and told me this story, thought that he was extremely conservative, when he had in fact taken enormous risks, had turned out to be completely wrong in his decisions, and was now in a position where recouping from the consequences of those errors was almost impossible. The main thrust of the argument is that you must be aware of *all* the risks you are taking, some of which are less obvious but no less important than others.

I consider "Is the Cult of the Equity Dead?" one of the most important pieces I have ever written. I say this in part because it deals with a most significant long-run trend among large investors—the decreasing proportion of money invested in fixed-income securities and the rising proportion of common stocks or of debt instruments with equity features attached. But it also gives me a chance to show how careful economic analysis can knock the stuffings out of a myth so widely held as to be considered gospel, so that it is an excellent example of my effort in this book to prove that you must think against the crowd if you seek the path to profit.

THE STRATEGY OF MODERN PENSION-FUND INVESTMENT*

In these chaotic times, how is anyone able to arrive at the cool, dispassionate, and prudent judgments that are so essential if we are to function successfully as fiduciaries? Managers of pension funds in particular have to deal with genuinely long-run objectives when the world is moving so fast that today gives very little hint as to what even tomorrow is going to be like.

---

* An address delivered at the Second Annual Conference on Employee Benefits sponsored by *Pension & Welfare News*, May 2, 1968.

My comments, observations, and suggestions, therefore, are made with real humility, for this is surely a moment when none of us can have any clear answers to the questions that plague us. I do feel, however, that the fundamental trends and forces in the American economy are less obscure than you might think at first glance. Furthermore, I believe that the investment requirements and objectives of pension funds are in many ways more appropriate to today's investment setting than the objectives of many other types of security portfolios. Finally, I think I can give you some basis for thinking against the crowd, for forming the objective and independent judgments that are absolutely essential for successful portfolio management.

In this paper, therefore, I shall deal in order with these three topics—the business outlook, the impact of economic developments on security prices, and the application of this forecast to the specific problems involved in pension-fund portfolio management.

Pension funds are managed within a framework of long-term investment decisions and are fundamentally different in character from a trading account or other types of portfolios with short-range objectives. In analyzing the economy, therefore, we would do well to look more at the forest than at the trees and to take a broader perspective than the day-to-day operator would take.

Seen from this viewpoint, the economy is likely to turn out to be less inflationary than it appears at the moment, especially if peace comes to Vietnam in the near future. This is real contrary thinking these days, when inflation is uppermost in most people's minds, but it deserves your most careful consideration.

I base this forecast in part upon a careful study of American economic history, which shows that intense inflationary episodes in our economy, although by no means nonexistent or infrequent, are nevertheless short-lived. I remind you that the cost of living has gone up by more than 2 percent in only eight out of the 21 years since 1946. Of those, six were associated with war—1947, 1948, 1951, 1952, 1966, and 1967; the rise in those years averaged better than 6 percent. Excluding these years, however, the 1946–1967 rise averaged less than 1.5 percent a year. The peacetime history of the United States shows a price trend that is a lot flatter than many people realize.

This should come as no surprise. Our economy is fabulously productive, remarkably flexible, and highly profit-oriented. Supply rises readily to meet demand. Rising costs stimulate the introduction of new techniques or lower-cost substitutes. Never underestimate the ingenuity of the American businessman in his breathless chase for the buck.

Furthermore, despite all the jokes to the contrary, our public policies *do* respond in varying degrees to inflationary pressures. Indeed, my main worry at the moment is that we will succumb to overkill in our efforts to extinguish the inflationary flames. The exigencies of the balance of payments in particular are forcing us into a more deflationary combination of policies than the purely domestic scene would otherwise justify.

In short, I suggest that you avoid being panicked by all the talk about inflation. It's here now, but it will diminish over the next couple of years. In fact, unless the war in Vietnam continues indefinitely and escalates from its current level, I would state flatly that an investment policy based on the premise of annual increases in living costs exceeding 3 percent over the long run will lead the portfolio manager to make some imprudent and costly mistakes.

In any case, if some of the wilder forecasts of inflation were to be true, I would warn you to go easy in the stock market. Once again, a study of history tells us that intense inflationary periods are poor times to own stocks and that the best times to own stocks are those when prices are relatively stable. Intense inflation brings on tight money, higher taxes, uncontrollable cost increases, and investment and inventory distortions, none of which is good for the stock market. They can ultimately lead to economic disaster. Even studies of countries like Brazil provide no assurance that the stock market is the right place to hedge against inflation. In Western Europe over the past five years, you would have lost less money in bonds than in stocks.

Of course, we are all well aware that there is a strong case to be made for common stocks. The record over the past 40 years or so shows that they have been supe-rior to bonds in their overall rate of return. In institutional portfolios, free of the need to liquidate assets and enjoying steady cash inflows, the greater volatility of common-stock prices represents an opportunity rather than a danger. Serious academic studies provide impressive data to support this position, while some highly conservative and respected financial institutions are carrying it into action by substantially reducing bond holdings and rapidly building up the equity portions of their portfolios.

However, before we go ahead and extrapolate these long-run results of the past into a long-run forecast of the future, we are at least justified in first asking whether some of the more unique characteristics of the past are likely to persist into the indefinite future. All of these long-run studies, while including the boom and bust of the late 1920s and the 1930s, also include the extraordinary phenomenon of the bull market that began in 1949.

This bull market has had a sweeping uptrend unmatched in our history. From 1871 to 1926, 11 significant downturns occurred in stock prices; after each high, an average of 56 months was required before the previous high was regained. The 1929 high stood unchallenged for more than 20 years. On the other hand, in the modest declines that we have experienced since 1949, the previous high has been regained on the average in about 15 months.

Furthermore, the upward path has not only been smoother but steeper as well. The rate of increase in stock prices since 1949 has been about four times the rate from 1871 to 1949. If we continued along at the old rate after

1949, stock prices today would be barely above the 1929 highs and we would have needed all these six years to recover from the 1962 break.

Since the law of change is the only immutable law of history, I am reluctant to accept the assumption that the record of the recent past can be mechanically projected into the future. A little skepticism is usually a good idea.

Please understand that I am not arguing against common stocks in a pension-fund portfolio. On the contrary, the slowness with which common stocks have been accepted and the consequent rush to join in the fun are now continual sources of amazement to me. Even if the upward trend in stock prices is going to be more gradual and bumpier than during the past 20 years, I still want to take advantage of the unique investment opportunities that common stocks offer to the pension-fund portfolio manager.

The only question, then, is not whether but how much?

This brings me, in fact, to the major thesis of this paper, which is to warn you against being sucked in by the present fad of going whole-hog and abandoning bonds wholesale to climb aboard the common-stock bandwagon.

As if anybody needs reminding of this fact, we live in a highly uncertain world. Forecasting is fun, but surely hazardous. Some people are right some of the time, but nobody is right all of the time and many of us are wrong most of the time. Maybe the bull market of the next 20 years will dwarf the present one. On the other hand, just because another great financial crash is unlikely, we would be fools to exclude the possibility completely. We simply don't know.

Yet, while we live in a world in which the future is largely unknown, trustees of pension funds have obligated themselves to pay a specific amount of money out to the beneficiaries at dates that do extend well out into the future. We have made an explicit promise to meet an obligation under future conditions that are essentially unpredictable. The important point, however, is that the promise is unconditional: It must be met.

Translated into portfolio-management terms, this tells us that, while we naturally would like to do better than the minimum requirements the actuaries have laid out for us, it would be fatal and catastrophic to fall short. The trustee who runs great risks in the hope of outperforming everything in sight is an extraordinarily irresponsible—but by no means nonexistent—man. Proper portfolio strategy for a pension fund necessitates limiting risks so that unexpected and unpleasant developments will in no way threaten the minimum objectives established by the actuaries. Such strictures may be unnecessary in profit-sharing funds or foundations or educational institutions or individual portfolios, where no contractual obligation exists. The crucial and determining consideration in the pension-fund portfolio is the contract that exists with the beneficiaries.

Seen from this point, the bond market today is a veritable cornucopia of goodies—just at the time when so many people are turning up their noses at it. It is especially tempting if my comments earlier about inflation turn out to be correct. Yields of better than 6½ percent are available on Aaa situations and much more is available to the portfolio manager with the energy and resources to seek it out. Here are contracts, legally enforceable contracts to pay, available at rates far in excess of the contract that exists between the fund and its beneficiaries. You are simply unable to avoid outperforming the actuarial requirement today if you just buy Aaa bonds. You can do a real job without any work at all.

In view of my basic premise that the future is unpredictable, however, I am afraid I can't make life quite that simple for you. For all the reasons you have heard here and elsewhere, common stocks *do* deserve a place in the portfolio and bonds *do* have their limitations. So you *do* have to work and worry.

However, the fat yields available on fixed-income investments can go far to reduce your worries, if not your workload. Since these yields are so far above the actuarial requirements, they give you that extra cushion of safety that both justifies and makes possible the opportunity to take risks in the hope of making big gains. If these ventures turn out badly, you recoup your losses from the extra income on your bonds; if they turn out well, you have it made.

This scheme fits perfectly my approach to common-stock investing. I am opposed to buying stocks for income or because the downside risks are small. I believe you should buy stocks in which you hope to make a killing, sometimes sooner, sometimes later. Often the psychological or financial circumstances of the client force me to compromise with this policy, but I pursue it as far as the clients will let me.

What I am saying, in short, is that a pension-fund portfolio with a large bond position at the present time is by no means a clear case of ultraconservatism—*the large bond position is the keel you need to enable you to hoist your common-stock sails high and venture into the open seas.*

This is a good spot to remind you of some obvious and simple but overwhelmingly important arithmetic: no common stock can decline by more than 100 percent but it always stands the chance of rising an infinite amount. Thus, your risk exposure is always measurable. If, then, common stocks are a minor portion of the portfolio at cost, the plump cushion of bond yields can offset your losses, while your gains can pull a lot of weight in measuring your performance if they really come through for you. This is why, I repeat, we believe this is the ideal structure that enables you to build an aggressive, high-performance common-stock portfolio.

While you are buying your bonds, incidentally, don't just put them away and forget them. If bonds make up half or more of your portfolio, that in itself justifies a good deal of attention. The bond market changes, too, and is full of interesting opportunities to play the yield curves, spreads between corporates and governments, and fundamental shifts in interest rates. We think that a bond portfolio always deserves aggressive management seeking out profit opportunities, but this is especially the case where a conscious strategic decision has been reached to allocate to it a substantial portion of the total funds invested.

We also think the convertible-bond market offers extraordinary opportunities at this particular moment, and we have replaced substantial amounts of straight bonds with convertibles in recent months. Just as an example— and there are many like this one—consider the American Airlines 4¼ of 1992, selling for 80. At this price, they yield 5.80 percent to maturity. Admittedly, this is at least 100 basis points less than one could get on a good straight bond of similar maturity today. However, these bonds would sell at par if American Airlines common got back to 47 from its present price in the high 20s; in fact, it sold above 40 during most of 1967. Don't you think it has a chance of getting back there before 1992, the maturity date of the bond? If it took until 1980, our yield to that date would be 6.70 percent if we then sold the bonds at par, thus matching in 12 years straight yields now available on 30-year bonds. If the common stock can get back to 47 anytime within the next seven years, our yield would exceed 8 percent. Not bad, in view of the small downside risk and the conservative assumptions we have made here.

If you were to ask me today what I think bond and stock prices will be a year from now, I would say I expect both of them to be higher. But this tells you only what I expect, not what is going to happen. If you ask me about five years out, I would admit that I just don't know what to expect, nor would I bet much money on anyone else's expectations.

While judgments about individual companies are easier to make, I still think that guessing the market is a treacherous basis on which to manage a portfolio. I have stressed here that pension-fund managers do know they have certain contractual obligations to meet and do know they can easily meet those obligations today in fixed-income investments that also rest upon contractual obligations. While we have hopes and expectations about common stocks, for both their yields and their dividends, we are still ignorant about what the actualities are going to be. I have never discovered any systematic relationship between what I think the market will do and what it actually does do.

Portfolio management is the art of relating investment decisions to capacities to assume risk and necessities to assume risk. *Risk* is the operative word, for it emphasizes our ignorance of the future. On the one hand, a pension fund's long-range character and continuous cash flow makes high-risk investments possible. On the other hand, the high yields available on fixed-income securities so far surpass the actuarial requirement that we have no necessity to take on large risks.

But it is precisely this combination of conditions that makes possible a rational portfolio policy for maximum return at minimum risk. We need not guess what security prices are going to do today, tomorrow, or next year. We anchor the portfolio safely with a substantial fixed-income position and then seek without worry to maximize our gains in an imaginative, aggressive, and fast-moving common-stock portfolio.

IS THE CULT OF THE EQUITY DEAD?*

No one would argue with the proposition that institutional investors are an important influence on the market for equities and that their influence is growing. Nor would anyone dispute the probability that institutions will have a continuously rising flow of billions to invest. Yet over the past seven years we had a net increase of less than a billion dollars a year in common stocks outstanding. Given the contrast between the growth in the size of institutional investment and the niggardly net increase in outstanding common stock available to buy, few people would doubt that a long-run shortage of common stocks lies ahead of us. How can we possibly satisfy the apparently voracious and insatiable appetite of these institutions for equities?

The answer to this question is obviously crucial in the formation of successful portfolio strategies. However, the conventional wisdom on the subject has hardly been questioned at all. Worse yet, the conventional wisdom

---

* From *Institutional Investor*, May 1970.

is based on extrapolation from the past, and the trouble with extrapolation is that it fails to recognize bends in the trends—or entirely new factors that can come into play as the future unfolds.

Let us begin with the projections recently published by the New York Stock Exchange. *Perspectives on Planning #5*, issued in January 1970 and entitled *The Demand for Corporate Equity: Projections to 1975 and 1980* (prepared by Professor Arnold E. Saffer of the Roth School of Business at Long Island University), projects a doubling of institutional demand for common stocks between 1968 and 1975 and a further increase of about 20 percent between 1975 and 1980. This study bases its forecast of growing institutionalization of the corporate equities market in the coming decade on these three assumptions:

1. "Increased institutional savings;
2. "Increased institutional incentive for equity investing;
3. "Reduction in the number of common stock offerings, as reflected by the fact that net new issues of corporate stock [have] supplied less than $1 billion of corporate funds annually."

I shall argue here on the other hand that the supply of new equities is going to be substantially *bigger* in the future than it has been in the past; that the "increased institutional incentive for equity ownership" is less certain than recent experience might suggest; and that the projected volume of net liquidation of common stocks by individual investors is even more difficult to determine. In short, it would appear that a long-run shortage of equities is essentially unpredictable; to the extent that it does occur, it is likely to be modest in size.

Let us begin the analysis by considering the probable future supply of new equities. Curiously, the Saffer study just cited devotes all of its attention to the demand side and makes no effort to arrive at an independent projection for supply; it uses a simple mechanical extrapolation of the recent experience when net supply has been way below institutional demand.

A reliable estimate of the future supply of equities rests upon one fundamental premise: If business activity in the United States is going to remain on a high level and to grow to even higher levels, the massive demands on our capital markets of the past few years will be much more of a permanent than a temporary phenomenon. (Of course, if business activity is *not* going to remain on a high level, or if we face an extended period of economic stagnation, then no one, including the institutions, is going to want to buy common stocks anyway.) We know that tremendous demands for funds exist and will persist among state and local governments and in the residential construction area. But business requirements for external financing are also going to be enormous if we retain a generally prosperous economy, in large part because business liquidity is now so low that internal cash flows are inadequate to finance expansion needs.

The numbers are impressive. Since 1962, sales of corporations have approximately doubled, but working capital has risen only one-third. In terms of liquidity as such, the situation is much tighter: cash and Governments at the end of 1969 were, at $63 billion, no higher than they had been at the end of 1962, while current liabilities soared from $171 billion to $325 billion. Over these seven years, the flow of gross retained earnings (total cash flow less dividends) rose less than 50 percent—and this was a time of impressive economic growth plus inflation—while total corporate debt nearly doubled.

No wonder, then, that external financing by corporations has shown such a dramatic uptrend. From 1960 to 1964, it averaged only $12.4 billion as sufficient liquidity remained to help cover corporate needs. In the next five years, however, the annual average of external financing was $28.7 billion, more than double the previous level. In 1969 alone, it ran to almost $40 billion.

Again on the assumption that we will have a prosperous economy, growth will continue to be financed externally to a very large extent because internal sources are simply inadequate to do the job. At $65 billion in 1969, gross retained cash flow was more than $10 billion short of plant and equipment expenditures alone, without even considering the financing of inventory, receivables, and foreign investment—or, indeed, without considering the desirability of rebuilding the deeply depleted residue of cash and governments. In other words, *liquidity has become a use for funds, rather than a source.*

Of course, the largest part of these needs will probably still come through debt rather than equity issues. Even at today's interest rates, interest is a deductible item while dividends have to be paid out of after-tax income. But two considerations suggest that equity financing will provide a higher proportion of funds than in the past.

First, as we have already seen, corporate debt has increased at a rate nearly twice as fast as the increase in gross retained earnings; this occurred during a period when profit growth was rapid by any historical standard of measurement and when burgeoning fixed-asset accounts and new tax benefits permitted an even stronger growth pattern for depreciation accruals. Consequently, many corporate treasurers are now counting their pennies a lot more carefully and are recalling Calvinist notions about the dangers of excessive use of debt—a viewpoint that is fully shared by lenders.

Second, while interest payments are admittedly tax-deductible, the margin between the cost of borrowing and the cost of equity money has narrowed in recent years. When the net cost of debt after taxes exceeds 4 percent and frequently brings with it restrictions on management's freedom of decision, the issuance of new shares of common stock begins to have its attractions, particularly since it brings in money that will never have to be repaid and that imposes no restrictions on management. Of course, this is irrelevant if we are going to have a permanently depressed stock market, but if that is what the future holds, talk about a shortage of common stocks is equally irrelevant. The analysis does suggest that new equity issues will come forth in volume in good markets as long as interest rates remain anywhere near current levels—and sharply lower interest rates would imply business conditions contrary to our basic assumption of continued prosperity.

But apparently the impetus to equity financing is so strong that it can persist even during poor market conditions. For example, the recent Standard Oil of New Jersey issue came along at a deeply depressed price. During the bear market year of 1969, in fact, total gross new cash stock offerings hit $7.9 billion, up from $4.1 billion in 1968, and equal to more than 70 percent of the *total* amount issued during the five-year period 1963–1967. Add another $2 billion for stock issued on options and for convertible bonds turned in for common stock, and you come up with the rather large sum of $10 billion in a year when market conditions were hardly buoyant.

But it is not only the historical standard of measurement that makes this figure loom large. First, $10 billion is not far from the volume of net new corporate bond issues in 1969, which amounted to $13 billion and which was, in fact, less than double the 1963–1967 annual average. Second, $10 billion is equal to at least 20 days of trading on the New York Stock Exchange at current levels of activity and in effect means that much money taken out of the market. Perhaps most significant of all, $10 billion is just about equal to total stock purchases by all nonbank investing institutions in 1969, which, as we shall see in more detail shortly, clearly raises some questions about the reputed shortage of common stocks.

Furthermore, this figure allows nothing for financing through convertible bonds, which had run comfortably below $2 billion a year through 1966 but then climbed to $4.5 billion in 1967, $3.3 billion in 1968, and close to $5 billion last year. This implies a substantial supply of new common stocks in the years ahead as these bonds are gradually converted by their holders. And, with interest rates remaining high, the likelihood is that convertible bond financing will continue to be heavy.

To some extent, the impact of new equity issues on the security markets has been diminished in recent years because of the takeover craze. Merger exchanges absorbed more than $2 billion in 1968 and 1969. However, the changed environment in Washington and the disappointing performance of the conglomerates will combine to reduce this influence in the years ahead. Furthermore, many shares of stock that disappeared through this route were replaced with convertible issues, so that their disappearance was only temporary, not permanent.

There is one additional factor that influences the net change in outstanding stock issues: corporate cash retirements of their own stock. This figure is by no means unimportant, as it jumps around between $2 billion and $4 billion. It is, however, trendless and really unpredictable. The most we can say about it is that it is likely to be a significant influence only when stock prices are low, as corporations would have little incentive to buy in their own stock when prices are high. Hence, to the extent that a shortage of common stocks may exist in the future and drive stock prices up, cash retirements will not do much to exacerbate the situation.

In summary, then, low liquidity, top-heavy levels of debt, and massive demands for money that will keep its cost high all suggest that the volume of new equity issues is going to remain on a lofty level and could even go higher. The days when we could talk of a potential shortage of equities because new supply was so small are dead and gone. Of course, all of this depends upon the validity of our assumption that we will continue to have a prosperous economy, but it is worth repeating that we can hardly expect to have a long-term bull market, regardless of the supply situation, in a depressed or stagnant economy.

But what about the demand side? What about those dizzying extrapolations of institutional demands for common stocks? Are there bends in those trends?

The patterns of net increase in ownership of corporate stock by financial institutions are curious, as the trends are more mixed than most people realize. And the significance of the figures is considerably more complex than most analysts of the subject have been willing to concede. Here is what the data look like:

Net Increase in Ownership	(Billions of dollars)							
	1962	1963	1964	1965	1966	1967	1968	1969
Savings Banks	0.1	0.1	0.1	0.2	0.0	0.2	0.3	0.3
Life Insurance Companies	0.3	0.2	0.5	0.7	0.3	1.1	1.4	1.4
Fire and Casualty Insurance Companies	0.2	0.1	0.1	0.1	0.4	0.6	1.1	-0.3
Private Noninsured Pension Funds	2.2	2.2	2.2	3.1	3.7	5.0	4.7	5.3
State and Local Retirement Funds	0.2	0.2	0.3	0.4	0.5	0.7	1.3	1.6
Open-End Mutual Funds	0.1	0.6	0.7	1.2	1.0	1.5	1.5	1.5
Total Nonbank Investing Institutions	3.1	3.4	3.9	5.7	5.9	9.1	10.3	9.8

SOURCE: Salomon Bros. & Hutzler.

NOTE: This analysis excludes foreign demand for U.S. equities. Although the figure was very large in 1968, its pattern is erratic and trendless. Any estimate of future demand would have to be too tentative to be useful.

And here is what Saffer's projections for these particular institutional investors look like for 1975:

	(Billions of dollars)
Savings Banks	0.2
Life Insurance Companies	3.9
Fire and Casualty Insurance Companies	0.9
Private Noninsured Pension Funds	11.1
State and Local Retirement Funds	1.2
Open-End Mutual Funds	6.8
Total	24.1

Saffer's past data and definitions differ somewhat from those used by Salomon Brothers, but the relationship between the general orders of magnitude (Saffer's total for 1968 is $10.7 billion) is sufficiently suggestive to indicate what enormous numbers you can derive by projecting past trends into the future.

Saffer makes his projections on the basis of two calculations. First, he estimates institutional net acquisitions of assets in future years. Second, he estimates the percent of institutional portfolios that will be held in the form of corporate equities. He cranks in a guess on market appreciation of equity prices (9 percent, naturally!), but that need not concern us here. Indeed, I see no need to quarrel for these purposes with his estimates of institutional asset growth. The important and crucial point is that most of his projections of the percent of institutional portfolios in the form of equities rise very steeply indeed as we go out into the future:

	Percent of Portfolios in Equities			
	1958	1963	1968	1975E
Savings Banks	2.3	2.4	2.7	2.5
Life Insurance Companies	3.9	5.2	7.8	17.7
Fire and Casualty Insurance Companies	34.2	37.1	42.0	50.0
Private Noninsured Pension Funds	41.2	52.0	64.4	80.0
State and Local Retirement Funds	?	3.9*	7.6	15.0
Open-End Mutual Funds	88.6	87.7	89.0	90.0

* 1964.

But I wonder how much reliance we can place on these 1975 projections when many of the factors at work in the past may have a very different look in the future.

In the first place, the patterns of net purchases by the fire and casualty companies surely point up the dangers of any kind of mechanical extrapolation. Note the completely flat trend from 1962 to 1965, the sharp upsurge between 1965 and 1968, and then the abrupt reversal to net liquidation in 1969. In estimating future purchases by these investors, shall we say that the trend is up, down, or sideways?

Second, since the largest institutional buyer of common stocks is the private noninsured pension fund group, the flattening-out in the trend of their net purchases of common stocks during the past three years is significant for the impact of total institutional demand on the equity market. With about two-thirds of their assets in common stocks already, it is difficult to understand why they should *accelerate* their purchases of common stocks in the future, as Saffer's data suggest is likely to happen. Indeed, in view of the competition that corporate bonds offer with yields that in most cases are double actuarial requirements, and with the increasing attraction of real-estate investments tied to equity kickers, one could argue that the proportion of pension-fund cash flow going into equities could just as easily stabilize or decline rather than increase.

On the other hand, the impressive rate of growth in state and local pension-fund buying of common stocks is likely to continue, because it starts from such a low base. However, the number of dollars involved here is still so small relative to the total that its impact on the overall demand for equities will be minor.

Life-insurance purchases of stocks showed a quantum jump in 1967, but the trend has been curiously sideways since then. Yet, given the great efforts now under way by major insurance companies to market equity instruments, their purchases of equities should rise rapidly, even if the Saffer estimate turns out to have been excessively optimistic.

The interesting question is not whether their purchases of stocks will expand but rather whether those increased purchases will be a *net* addition to the demand for common stocks. One could argue that some of the common stocks that the life insurance companies will purchase with their customers' money are stocks that the customers would have bought on their own if they had not entrusted those particular funds to the insurance salesman.

This question relates even more directly to the figures on purchases by open-end mutual funds. During the 1940s and 1950s, these funds unquestionably attracted money into equities that would otherwise have gone into savings banks, United States savings bonds, or ordinary life insurance. Today, however, the American family is used to the idea of owning common stocks; those who suffer from the phobia of 1929-itis are no longer a significant number among the buyers of securities. The issue in most households today is how to go about building and managing a common-stock portfolio, rather than *whether* to own one at all.

What this means, in short, is that a major portion of mutual-fund demand and an indeterminant but probably meaningful share of life insurance demand is really a substitute for individual demand rather than a net increase in the demand for common stocks. We shall pursue this matter shortly in our discussion of individual demand.

The analysis does suggest that the impact of institutional ownership is complicated to project. Although the tremendous increase in turnover among institutional portfolios has greatly increased their share of daily trading, this is something quite different from measuring their *net* purchases. The figures show an impressive rise during the 1960s, but most of it was accomplished by 1967. What we really want to know is whether the flat trend since 1967 is just a pause or an indication of things to come. And to what extent are institutional purchases replacing and to what extent are they complementing individual investment? No one at this point can be sufficiently certain of the answers to these questions to be able to make any kind of a reliable estimate of the total demand for common stocks three, four, five, or ten years down the road, even though the temptation to do so is still a fashionable pastime.

The decisions and capabilities of individual investors with respect to the ownership of common stocks are obviously crucial. Despite the much-vaunted institutional accumulation of common stocks over the past 20 years or so, individuals still hold about $500 billion in this form, nearly 80 percent of the total and more than 60 percent even if we switch common and personal trusts from the individual to the institutional category. This is indeed a vast reservoir to supply institutional requirements.

To what extent can we expect individual investors to be net sellers in the years ahead? We do know that they liquidated on balance an annual average of about $4 billion during the first half of the decade, but this built up to the substantial figure of $13.5 billion in 1968 and remained at the relatively high level of nearly $8 billion in 1969.

An important segment of individual liquidation is involuntary, primarily to provide the necessary cash for the payment of estate, gift, and capital gains taxes. An indeterminate but important amount flows each year as gifts to

charities and educational institutions, who in turn liquidate most of what they receive in this form. The balance,
of course, is subject to the attitudes of individuals toward
owning common stocks.

Two important factors are likely to have a significant
influence on the attitudes of individual investors toward
common stocks: the need and desire for professional
asset management on the one hand, and the attraction of
competing forms of investment on the other. Both tend
toward an increasing rate of individual liquidation.

The desire for professional asset management stems
both from the probability that the commission cost of
small transactions is going to go much higher and from
the widely held belief that professionals can do a better
job of investing than individuals can do by themselves.
Those of us who earn our livings as money managers may or may not agree with this viewpoint, but there
is no doubt that, despite the ravages of the 1969 market
on many performance records, the professional money
manager has acquired a glamorous aura similar to that
enjoyed by psychoanalysts, brain surgeons, and astronauts.
The aggressive merchandising of the investment advisory
industry and its role in the management of billions of dollars of fiduciary and educational money leads the individual increasingly in the direction of letting the pros take
care of things for him. The rude discovery in 1969 that
stocks are *not* a hedge against inflation did nothing to help
the individual investor's self-respect.

The second factor that will tend to make individuals liquidate more common stock (or to buy less) is the growing attraction of alternative investments. The bond market is a striking case in point. According to Salomon Brothers & Hutzler, individuals invested $25 billion in open market debt securities in 1969, about 75 percent more than in the credit crunch period of 1966 and nearly three times as much as in 1968. In a market that had been almost entirely institutional, the individual investor has now become a major factor. There is no reason for him to go away as long as bond yields remain so much higher than the income available on common stocks and on savings deposits.

Real estate has become another competing investment outlet. The attractive return available, the traditional role of real estate as an inflation hedge, and the comfort in owning something you can kick with your foot have all brought a new and growing interest into the real estate field. A variety of instruments have been created to satisfy this need, as exemplified by the proliferation of real-estate investment trusts or the type of real-estate mutual fund being offered by Connecticut General. All of this will be drawing away funds that might otherwise have gone into the stock market.

Thus, the lure of the bond market, a new look to real estate, the attraction of professional money management, and disillusion at the ability of common stocks to provide a good hedge against the inflationary pressures of 1969 have all combined to make individual ownership of common stocks less attractive than it was. If this is so, the great pool of individual holdings can be pried loose by institutions more readily: that is, without the necessity to drive prices up so much.

In this connection, it is worth having another look at the Saffer study. A most intriguing and important phenomenon appears in the presentation in his statistical appendix: Individuals have held their corporate equities, figured at market value, to the narrow range of 42.4 percent to 46.5 percent of their total financial assets ever since 1958. Net liquidation, in other words, has just about offset appreciation over a full decade.

Now Saffer predicts that individuals will want to continue to hold about 45 percent of their total financial assets in the form of corporate equities. He takes his projection of the growth of individual asset holdings and his projection of rising market values of equities and then, by applying this 45 percent figure to the result, he comes out with the enormous figure of $27.9 billion of net liquidation by individual investors in 1975, more than double the rate in 1968 and almost quadruple the annual average from 1963 through 1968. The figure is so large, in fact, that it actually *exceeds* his projection of total institutional demand of $27.1 billion in 1975 (which includes $3.0 billion of nonprofit institutions in addition to the groups in the tables on pages 203 to 205).

While one could take issue with Saffer's methodology, the implications of his analysis, taken together with the factors we have already discussed, are decidedly bearish. If individual liquidation so completely satisfies institutional demand, who will buy those billions of dollars of new issues that seem destined to hit the market in the years ahead?

Perhaps this analysis has been too open-ended for the fellow who has to have precise numbers for 1975 and 1980. But that is precisely the point: Projections of a long-run shortage of common stocks have zero reliability, because the unknowns are much greater than the practitioners of such simplified estimates are willing to recognize. As we have just seen, one could even build a case that equities are going to be in a condition of oversupply, but even that case is too tenuous for long-range planning.

What this does tell us, then, is that the fundamentals of supply and demand—and particularly demand—are too uncertain to help us predict the future trend of the market. The long-term bulls will have to look elsewhere to make their case.

HAVE YOU MET MR. JONES?*

Risk is a primary consideration in investment decisions, the constant companion of every venture, and the ultimate determinant of investment success. But while most of us who buy securities are aware of the necessity to

_____

* A Bernstein-Macaulay bulletin, September 1, 1964.

consider risk in the individual items we select, few people give sufficient thought to the relation between risk and their entire portfolio—and even fewer to the degree to which risk in other aspects of their lives can and finally must profoundly influence the structure and the results of their investment program.

A story recently related to us by a friend in another financial organization is a dramatic illustration of the truth of this statement. We therefore repeat the essentials of the story here, although we have, of course, changed certain details to protect the identity of the subject.

Mr. Jones was in his mid-fifties, was married, and had a child approaching college age. Although he was in a well-regarded and profitable profession, his work absolutely required the constant use of his eyes. As the result of a gradual but nevertheless progressive disease, he was now unable to use his eyes as much as the nature of his work required. Consequently, his income was slowly but steadily shrinking as his clientele moved elsewhere. He had no other skills, nor any interest at this point in acquiring them. Neither he nor his wife had given any thought to her taking up an activity to supplement the family income.

Mr. Jones and his wife had saved up over the years about $75,000. While $75,000 is a lot of money to accumulate just out of income in these days of high prices and progressive tax rates, the income on it would be far below even this family's modest standard of living, and far too little to finance the son's advanced education besides.

With about 20 years' life expectancy, these people would either have to undertake a drastic revision of their entire way of life or face the unpleasant possibility of outliving their money. They were indeed badly in need of a miracle man rather than an investment counselor.[*]

Mr. Jones maintained that he had always been "a most conservative guy" and stressed repeatedly how his financial conservatism would make the taking of risks most difficult to accept, even if the objective circumstances were more favorable to it. And, with the consequences of loss disastrous at this stage of the game, the circumstances were hardly favorable.

But the maddening touch to this story is that Mr. Jones had taken enormous risks in his life, had lost on all of them, and now sought some impossible magic formula to bail him out.

Had he life insurance with cash values? No, all his insurance was group insurance with his professional association and could conceivably expire if he retired from active work. Had he disability insurance to cover just such a situation as this? No. Had he made any effort to take in a younger man as a partner who could now take over his clientele and give him a share of the receipts? Never. Had his wife shown any interest in acquiring a skill or

---

[*] Despite some widely held, popular misconceptions and some occasional brief indications to the contrary, these are two different professions.

some knowledge that would supplement his income if he were ill? No sign of it.

His independence, self-assurance, and good earning power had encouraged him to a boldness in assuming risks that, in retrospect, appears almost incredible (although by no means unusual). If he had carried straight life insurance, purchased disability insurance, taken in a younger man with whom he would have had to share his income, and encouraged his wife to pursue her education, he would probably have less than $75,000 in the savings bank today—but he would really be in far better shape. Together with these other sources of assured income, the return on his savings would doubtless come close to covering his needs. To the extent that he had to dip into principal, he could do so with a lighter heart.

Because he had taken none of these precautionary steps, he had in effect assumed one colossal risk: that his own earning power would be large enough and would last long enough to provide comfortably for his family until they were so old that they no longer had any chance of outliving their capital. The boldest gambler at the poker table is unwilling to face odds like these—or, if he does, he refuses to stake everything on them. There was too little to win in relation to what he could lose.

Mr. Jones was clearly a lot less conservative than he thought he was. Indeed, his temerity in running the rest of his life had *forced* him into an unnecessary and, in retrospect, unfortunate degree of conservatism in the management of his savings. If he had moved to protect the family's income against the hazards of illness and age, he could have taken greater risks with his savings and purchased some common stocks in preference to stuffing the vaults of the savings banks. Over the period of this man's working years, even fair success in the stock market could have been highly profitable. Thus, even though he might have added less to his savings out of his own earnings because of the protection he bought, he probably would have come out with as much money as or more money than he has today.

While we have turned a phrase in the title of this bulletin, our purpose has been more than just to be witty. In the course of our work, we frequently meet people like Mr. Jones. Our hunch is that most of us know more people like Mr. Jones than we realize, and that occasionally we meet these Mr. Joneses by looking in the mirror. Few people ever face risk—its necessities and its consequences—either honestly or consistently. Like the billiard player who twists his body in the hope that it will somehow transmit a change in direction to a ball already rolling, we tend to use body English on some of our decisions and consequently have to overhedge on others.

Human nature being what it is, most people, like Mr. Jones, learn this lesson too late in life. But we must admit that it adds great zest to our own work, for no investment decision involving risk can be made without just such an analysis as this. Within the context of our tasks, we find much more than arithmetic to worry about.

NOTES ON PORTFOLIO PLANNING*

If the future were known, investment counseling would have no excuse for existing. But, for better or for worse, the investment process consists of making decisions for a future that is always uncertain. Thus, risk—the possibility that events may turn out differently from the way one expects—is an unwanted but inescapable companion in portfolio management. While every investor obviously wants to make as much money as possible, he must select his approach to that objective with full consideration of the consequences that investment errors might mean to him.

We believe that this line of analysis leads to investment programs that are much more meaningful and effective than the conventional breakdown of investment objectives among income, safety, and capital appreciation. Concentration on any one of these objectives can be extremely costly. The search for high income may necessitate taking risks so excessive that capital losses will offset income gained; an obsession with safety of principal runs the risk that the purchasing power of that principal may be lost in an inflationary period; and securities selected only for growth have an annoying habit of going sharply in reverse from time to time.

Thus, the choice of just one investment objective—income, safety, or capital appreciation—involves such large

---

* A Bernstein-Macaulay bulletin, May 1, 1965.

risks because of the exclusion of the other two that its achievement is probably impossible. Of course, simultaneous achievement of all three would be ideal—everyone would like to maximize his assets and purchasing power without incurring losses in the effort to do so. But this is also impossible.

Investment planning must therefore recognize from the start that we have no way of avoiding the possibility that events may turn out differently from the way we expect and that our choice of securities may fail to serve the purposes for which they were selected. In the light of this, what distinguishes one investor's portfolio from another's is the degree to which the maximizing process must be tempered by the consequences of loss and error. These are the fundamental considerations that will shape the structure of the portfolio and the individual securities it contains.

That is why we begin portfolio planning with an analysis of the investor's capacity to take risks and with an examination of the consequences of investment errors to his financial (and psychological) security. This involves not only the magnitude of losses but the flexibility that is essential if the losses are to be recouped. Questions of age, insurance, family responsibilities, job security, cash reserves, and so on are designed both to determine how much risk the investor can afford to take (and should take) as well as to define the staying power that will enable him to avoid the awful necessity to liquidate and pull out when security values are depressed. Investment can be successful only when liquidation is at a time of the investor's own choosing rather than *force majeure.*

Once we see that investment is a process of maximizing assets and purchasing power with due regard to the consequences of loss, portfolio planning is made simpler and, indeed, can be much more varied. For example, why should the so-called widows-and-orphans type of account be denied the advantages of capital appreciation offered by growth stocks when such opportunities arise? If these stocks involve higher risk and lower income, then they should be bought in only limited amounts, but that is no reason to exclude them: Every investor should have at least some position in those securities he or his advisor judges to be the most promising at any moment in time.

In another instance, why should the businessman eschew the high return available on tax-exempt bonds just because his earned income is large enough to sustain the standard of living he desires or just because he can afford to assume the risks inherent in common stocks? Unspent income is an addition to capital—it increases one's assets in an even better way than appreciation, because it is surer (and, through municipal bonds, can be tax-free besides). Thus, while our businessmen clients stress to us their desire for growth in contrast to income, we point out to them that capital can be enhanced through additional income as well as through appreciation and with substantially less risk that the objective will fail of achievement.

On the same line of reasoning, we have little use for the conventional designations of common stocks as "income stocks," "defensive stocks," "growth stocks," and, of all things, "businessman's risk stocks." The purpose of investment is to maximize return and assets with due regard to the risks involved; since it is in the nature of common stocks to involve the greatest degree of risk, we see no point at all in buying them other than with expectations of substantial capital appreciation. In today's security markets, risk considered, fixed-income investments provide significantly greater income than common stocks. The purchase of a "defensive" common stock that one hopes will not go down is a distortion of emphasis: Safety of principal is better secured in fixed-income investments. The only attraction in common stocks today is the promise of capital appreciation, but the proportion of the total portfolio invested in common stocks and the quantity of any individual issue the investor buys must be limited by the probabilities that his expectations of future events could turn out to be wrong.

Since the future always can—and frequently does—develop differently from the way one expects, we try to avoid extreme positions whose success depends upon a completely correct forecast: To sell out, to be 100 percent in the market, to maintain a top-heavy position in one issue all imply an ability to forecast the future that Nostradamus himself did not have. These are also positions in which the consequences of being wrong can be disastrous. To the extent that they are undertaken, they must be hedged out in other aspects of the investor's finances or even his way of life.

Indeed, we repeat that the consequences of being wrong are the most vital considerations in portfolio planning. The most important question an investor can ask himself is the extent to which his family's present and future living standards would be affected by a change in the value of his securities. This is where the measurement of risk-taking capacity must begin. Where a drastic shrinkage in capital would have a significant impact on the family's daily life and also where a substantial appreciation in capital would have little influence on the way they live, we see no justification for heavy positions in common stocks; where, on the other hand, the consequences of loss are minor but substantial gains could provide a real improvement in present or future living standards, we favor an aggressive investment program.

Portfolio planning, in short, begins with a premise of humility, but its strategy and tactics offer large rewards.

HOW NOT TO LOSE MONEY ON TAX SWITCHES*

An accountant and a tax consultant are two things that an investment counselor is not. Yet, since most of his clients think that he is (among other things that they occasionally

---

* A Bernstein–Macaulay bulletin, November 1, 1965. Some data revised.

think he is), we are inevitably caught up in the annual whirling-dervish rites of offsetting capital gains with losses and offsetting losses with gains.

In our experience, we have found that much of this feverish activity is foolishness, resulting in unwise investment selections, unnecessary expenses, and waste motion. Here, then, are a few hints that are a little different from the run-of-the-mill tax-switching advice that will soon be flooding the mails and the financial columns.

1. Don't Have Delusions of Grandeur

Many people exaggerate the size of the capital-gains tax they will have to pay. In its crudest form, this delusion even goes so far as the belief that the tax will be 35 percent of the total price received for a stock, when, of course, only the profit is taxed. And, in a great many cases, the tax on the profit will work out to less than 35 percent.

The long-term capital-gains tax is figured as follows: *Half* of your net long-term gains are added to your regular income and therefore taxed at your top bracket. To put it another way, we can say that the tax on long-term profits will be half your top bracket less the deduction for long-term losses.

But this means that the capital-gains tax today will be less than 35 percent, unless your net taxable income (total taxable earnings from all sources less all exemptions and deductions) is above $44,000, or unless the size of your profits pushes it above that figure. A married couple paying tax on, say, $15,000 would pay about $3,200 in income taxes if they had no capital gains; if they established $6,000 in net long-term gains, they would pay tax on $18,000 ($15,000 + 50 percent of their profit), which would come to $4,100. Thus, the tax incurred on account of the gain would be only $900, or 15 percent rather than the maximum of 35 percent. A couple with net taxable income as high as $30,000 taking $10,000 in long-term gains would pay a tax of $2,100 on account of the profit—less than 35 percent.

2. Don't Make Your Broker Rich

Tax switching costs money. The broker takes about 1 percent on each sale and purchase; in addition, most sales are made on the bid price in the market while buyers pay up to the offer price.

Take a man who had bought 100 shares of stock at 50; it is now 45, and he wants to sell it to offset a gain that would otherwise be taxed at 20 percent. So he sells it, establishes his loss of $500, purchases a different stock for 45, and figures he has saved $100 in capital-gains taxes. He has saved $100 in taxes, all right, but he has also paid out $83 in brokerage! This procedure assumes particularly ridiculous proportions when, as frequently happens, the loss was the only reason he had for selling the stock in the first place.

In typical cases where we do the arithmetic, and especially where the investor's gains are taxed at less than

35 percent, establishing losses of less than 10 points saves so little, net after brokerage expenses, that the best decision is to leave well enough alone.

3. Don't Sell Pearls to Buy Paste

The greatest foolishness of all in this silly season is the desire of so many investors, aided and abetted by carefully constructed lists published by brokers and advisory services, to replace a stock sold at a loss by another stock that *must* be in the same industry, selling at the same price, and, if at all possible, just as depressed as the one being sold. This desire seems to exist even when the stock being sold is far superior to the one being bought, or when the investor may be well rid of an ailing company in a lagging industry, and when nothing is more irrelevant to investment success than the search for a stock you can buy at $30 simply because you just sold something at that price.

Our ultimate purpose in all of this is to regain what was lost on a bad investment. A sale produces free uncommitted cash: You should in turn commit that cash to any investment, anywhere, at any price that shows the best chance of achieving your objective in investing in the first place, which is to maximize your return.

Chapter 7

PHILOSOPHY AND FANTASY

The reader will find less of economics and finance in this section and rather more of my view of life as a whole.

I happen to be an activist with a concern for the welfare of the community. Sometimes I think we put the welfare of the individual a little too far ahead of the community. This leads to the establishment of values that seem false to me—but I also believe that we can revise those values and that we can accomplish something in meeting the needs of the community.

The first essay in this section is a defense—three years after the fact—of the thesis set forth in my first book, *The Price of Prosperity*. The argument in essence was that government spending (even if accompanied by higher taxes) is a stimulant rather than an inhibitor of growth, that more government may be better than less government, and that better schools and streets are more necessary than bigger television sets and automobiles.

While I wrote the book during 1961 and in October 1964 made the defense of it that is reproduced here, the whole argument has an ironic twist to it as I write this in the spring of 1969. We got the big additional load of government spending after 1964, all right, and a rate of economic growth more rapid than the most optimistic predictions of the Soaring Sixties had envisaged—but we got it to pay for the destruction of Vietnam rather than to build schools and streets at home. World War II and the Vietnam War have both proven that government spending can, in fact, bring us to full employment and a rapid rate of economic growth, but the question that keeps nagging at me (and is posed explicitly in the last chapter of *The Price of Prosperity*) is why only the military can push Congress to step on the accelerator.

Hopefully, we may now be moving into a period when the Pentagon will be the poor man of the government and when pressures for high levels of spending for community projects will be strong enough to assure us of a gross national product (GNP) that may be expanding quantitatively for sure but qualitatively as well. Some satirical comments on this approach are set forth in the final essay, "An Immodest Proposal," which appeared June 1, 1967.

This requires some brief comment on the essay that precedes it, "A Modest Proposal," which appeared September 1, 1958. Although I wish I had written this extraordinary piece, I did not. It was written by my late partner, Linhart Stearns, who had a fine touch for this kind of satire; I have included it here as sort of a memorial to him, but also because of its unusual quality. It has lost none of its relevance with the passage of time. It was so persuasive when it first appeared, in fact, that it brought us a denial, in all seriousness, from the then Undersecretary of the Treasury for Monetary Affairs.

"THE PRICE OF PROSPERITY"— INFLATED OR DEFLATED?*

Just about two years ago, Humphrey Neill, in his "Letter of Contrary Opinion," was good enough to urge his subscribers to read my recently published book, *The Price of Prosperity.* He did say that "the book will make you mad in spots," he confessed to writing "Ouch" in the margin in any number of places, he referred to "distasteful" opinions in it, and concluded his review by saying, "I shan't upset you further with this annoying book"—but then he added the phrase that I liked best: "You best ask your book-seller for it."

But he must be a sucker for punishment, because now he has invited me up here to say my piece in person.

---

* An address delivered at the Second Annual Contrary Opinion Forum, Stratton, Vermont, sponsored by Fraser Management Associates, Inc., October 2, 1964.

Perhaps I am easier to get at in flesh than on paper, but, in any case, I expect that Mr. Neill will still be saying "Ouch" and will still be mad when I am through today. For I strongly believe that the passage of time since my book appeared, in the spring of 1962, has vindicated the position that it took and has only served to strengthen my own convictions that I was on the right track.

Let me summarize briefly what the book was about and what it had to say.

The central problem that concerned me was the inescapable necessity for American businessmen to create twice as many additional jobs during the 1960s as they had created during the highly prosperous decade of the 1950s. As a result of the low birth rates of the 1920s and 1930s, the economy of the 1940s and 1950s was characterized by a relative shortage of people of working age. But, as a consequence of the rising birth rates of the 1940s and 1950s, we are now moving abruptly into a period when the number of people of working age will be rising far more rapidly than at any time since the great waves of immigration 60 years ago or more.

The relative shortage of labor that we have experienced over the past 20 years was directly related to the extraordinarily sharp rise in wage rates that accompanied it. This development was by no means all bad, however. High and rising wages stimulated working people to borrow and spend money freely and thereby to keep the wheels of industry turning—and, consequently, to keep the demand for labor strong. Furthermore, businessmen were required to spend enormous sums on new and more efficient types of plant and equipment, which, in turn, meant a high level of investment, more demand, and more jobs. The upward sweep of wage rates, in other words, gave an important and persistent push to the willingness of both consumers and businessmen to go out and spend money.

In this present decade, the number of people entering the labor force will be twice as great as it was in the 1950s. In the 1970s, it will be even greater. Unless automation or other forms of productivity improvement should suddenly come to a halt or slow down significantly, we are going to have a hard time indeed finding jobs for all these war babies and postwar babies and post-postwar babies as they grow up. Even if the demand for goods and services expands as rapidly as it did during the great surge of postwar prosperity from 1947 to 1957, my book projected a heavy load of unemployment at the end of the decade. In short, without a strong and unwavering sense of urgency about spending money in these years, the unemployment figures are going to continue to be a disturbing blot on our affluent society.

However, not only do I doubt whether such powerful motivations to spend money are likely to be present, but the sudden shift from labor shortage to labor surplus may actually dampen such urgency as does exist. The law of supply and demand tells us, and experience teaches us, that prices fall or at least rise more slowly when supply expands faster than demand. We can therefore expect—as we have already begun to witness in the past couple of years—a distinct moderation in the rate of wage increases. Wages are still rising, admittedly—but the really big jumps in wage rates are clearly a phenomenon of the past, not the present.

But now we see a mirror image of the previous set of circumstances. If wages are rising more slowly and if the unemployment rolls are rising rapidly, will consumers be such urgent borrowers and spenders, and will businessmen find it so necessary to sink money into capital goods designed to economize on labor? In short, while a fully prosperous economy requires a tremendous acceleration in the demand for goods and services, the very increase in the supply of workers may serve to thwart the expenditures needed to provide the jobs they seek.

In the absence of other types of adjustments, then, I have doubted whether the private sectors of the economy could possibly increase their spending enough to absorb these new workers and avoid the social and political tensions that would result from excessive unemployment. The only solution that I could find to this dilemma was to urge a substantial expansion of the public sector, whose rising expenditures would create new jobs, raise the incomes of the private sectors, and, as highly desirable by-products, give us the better roads, schools, and urban centers that we so desperately need. This is the point, as you have probably guessed, where Humphrey Neill began to write "Ouch" in the margins.

Now that we stand full stride in the middle of the 1960s and now that the first crop of those war babies has reached the age of 18, how does this analysis look?

Here are a few figures to show you what has been going on. The labor supply—the number of people either at work or seeking work—increased by 800,000 people a year from 1957 to 1962. But in the past two years it has increased by an annual rate of 1.3 million. In the next two it will increase by nearly two million a year. The rise in hourly wage rates in recent years has slowed down to only about 3 percent a year—half of what it was during the 1950s. Indeed, labor cost per unit of output is not only lower than it was last year or the year before, but lower than it has been at any time in more than eight years!

While the wage agreements just reached in the automobile industry may appear to be a reversal of this trend, I think we have obscured their real significance. Many other industries will be unable to meet and will refuse to meet wage demands of this magnitude. More important, the automobile settlements are consistent with the current trend in labor relations toward provisions for job security and early retirement—both of which are directly related to the environment of excessive unemployment.

For the unemployment figure has hovered around 5 percent of the labor force over the past 18 months, even though the GNP has been rising at the unusually rapid rate of about 6 percent a year. As usual, unemployment is concentrated among the young, the unskilled, and the minorities. We are all too painfully familiar with this fact for me to linger on it. We don't need any statistics to tell us about it, for the violence that has disturbed our cities this summer is a direct manifestation of what I am talking about.

Our failure to bring the unemployment figure down to socially tolerable levels during a period of unusually rapid economic growth convinces me that the problem posed in my book is one of desperate seriousness. For the growth in the number of people seeking jobs is only just beginning, and economic expansion at its current swift pace is seldom sustained indefinitely. In short, we have only just begun to see the nature of the troubles that lie ahead of us.

But what about solutions? If, as the past year has demonstrated, vigorous growth in the private sector is inadequate to sop up the pool of unemployed, I see no alternative to further stimulation from governmental fiscal policy. This should take the form of either tax cuts without reductions in government spending or more spending without any increase in the tax burden.

Let me emphasize that tax cuts accompanied by reductions in government spending may sound attractive but in reality solve nothing. Tax cuts leave more purchasing power in the pocket of the taxpayer. But cuts in spending take purchasing power away from those who were living on the government payroll. If government spending must be cut back as fast as we reduce the tax burden, we must be willing to spend out of our own pockets *more* than the amount we are saving in taxes. Otherwise, we shall have had a shift in demand from the public to the private sector but no net increase in the demand for goods and services, and, consequently, in the demand for labor. Perhaps the reduction in government spending will make so many people happy that they will, in fact, go out and spend more than they saved through the tax cut, but I see nothing in the experience of this country to guarantee that this will be the result. On the contrary, I am afraid that we will spend *less* than the tax cut, so that the corresponding reduction in government spending will mean a net loss of jobs rather than a gain.

Therefore, my own unshakable and highly contrary opinion favors more government spending rather than tax cuts. Then I am sure the money will be spent and certain that the jobs will be created. Of course, I recognize that many people are alarmed at the prospect of steadily expanding federal-government expenditures. I shall address only two questions to them.

First, do you realize that, after adjustment for price increases, federal-government nondefense expenditures today are *less* than they were in the years just before World War II? In other words, outside the defense sector, the federal government today is actually contributing only a tiny bit to the demand for goods, for services, and for labor.

Second, is there any loss of freedom to Americans in the better schools, better roads, better housing, better hospitals, better flood control and irrigation, better recreation facilities, and better conservation of our natural resources that greater federal government expenditures can help us to achieve? The threat to our freedom is to be found in the lawlessness that springs from unemployment and social frustration, not in the size of the federal budget.

But, the rejoinder will come, what about inflation? Shouldn't we worry about the dollar going down the drain?

To be completely contrary, I suppose I should shrug off the inflation problem. So foolish I am not. Yet I wonder whether we are not more foolish—or perhaps I should say foolhardy—to exaggerate the inflation nightmare to the point where we resist stimulation from fiscal policy. For one thing, I find social violence and the breakdown of law and order infinitely more frightening and disturbing than a couple of percentage points in the cost-of-living index. If some inflation is the price of opening up economic opportunity to the underprivileged, then I am willing to pay that price.

But I doubt whether we have to set the choice in those terms. The American economy, despite all the myths to the contrary, is remarkably inflation-resistant. We can't boast about our extraordinary productivity on the one hand and worry too much about inflation on the other. Except under the abnormal conditions of wartime, supply catches up with demand with amazing rapidity in our economy. Ask any businessman whether it is easy to raise prices in an economy as competitive and dynamic as ours. With the substantial amount of excess capacity that still exists after the capital-goods boom of the late 1950s and with the tremendous new wave of capacity expansion now under way, to say nothing of the rapidly rising supply of labor, I see little likelihood of inflation here in the years ahead—or, at least, little likelihood of inflation at a rate to justify a deflationary bias to fiscal policy.

Furthermore, the greatest mistake we can make about inflation is to associate it solely with governmental financial operations. Inflation comes about when demand is excessive relative to supply. Sometimes this results—as in wartime—when the government fills our pockets too full of money either by spending too much or taxing us too little. But sometimes—as in 1956, 1957, or 1960—prices rise despite federal surpluses because the demand for private goods and services is excessive relative to the supply.

This is an extremely important point, seldom stressed, that justifies some elaboration. Therefore, let me go further with it.

Unless business is good in the years to come—unless business is, in fact, very, very good—we will never be able to reduce unemployment to manageable levels. But if a level of business activity sufficiently vigorous to eliminate excessive unemployment does result in inflation, then we shall have inflation whether the stimulus to the economy comes from fiscal policy or from rapid expansion of consumer and business spending.

Remember that the solution to the unemployment problem depends upon unusually good business conditions. Remember, too, that inflation is the consequence of good business, not of depression. The businessman who finds he is able to sell more than he can produce will raise his prices. He will not stop to ask his customers whether their eagerness to buy his merchandise is the result of money the government has put in their pockets or the result of money their employers have put in their pockets. He will raise prices because he thinks he can get away with it, and he thinks he can get away with it because business is good. And, to complete the circle, unless business is good, we are going to have to face the nightmare of unemployment.

But I must repeat that our economic history tells us that the prospects for peacetime inflation are small, even during periods of rapid growth. The dangers we face in minimizing the inflation problem are much less than the risks we run in overemphasizing it.

Let us rather look at the problem in the broader context of the good society in which we are lucky enough to live. As free-spending consumers, we have enjoyed steadily rising living standards. As bold and creative investors, we have built a fabulously productive industrial base. We are going to grow in the years to come, and our living standards will rise. What I fear is not that we shall fail to grow, but that we shall fail to grow fast enough, that our traditional hunger for more goods and for better ways of producing them will be insufficient. We are about to reap the whirlwind of the baby boom we have supposedly enjoyed in the years since the war: As the baby boom forced adjustments within our private lives, we must now face equally great adjustments in our view of the public sector, whose additional growth we shall need to help make jobs for all those babies who, unlike Peter Pan, must inevitably grow up.

This is not a problem in ice-cold economics, nor is it a problem just for those families unfortunate enough to figure in the unemployment statistics. For the first time in more than 30 years, this country has had a taste of social revolution and violence. Where for so many years we have looked with detachment at newspaper pictures of the faces of furious mobs of foreigners, we now see the faces of fellow Americans. I do not like these pictures. Nor do I want us to solve this problem by a police state that brooks no opposition, no controversy, no contrary opinions. Rather, I hope that we can find the solution in the typically American way, by creating an environment in which no one has any cause to respond to incitements to violence and revolution.

IS WORK NECESSARY?*

Is unemployment part of the human condition—or is it a brainchild of the statisticians? Although fewer than 70 million out of a total of 190 million American citizens are actually working today, no one claims that 120 million people are unemployed. Some of those 120 million are too young to work; some are too old; some are sick; some are enjoying the fruits of affluence and don't have to work; some are housewives, tending homes and children; some are at school; some are in the armed forces. By the latest count, only about four million people are actually seeking jobs and unable to find them.

This suggests an intriguing flight of fancy into a utopian world in which we eliminate unemployment simply by persuading four million people to stop working! Let us suggest to them that they choose instead to go back to school, enjoy early retirement, or stay home and spend more time with their children or parents.

Fanciful as this idea may seem, and despite all of the practical obstacles to it that at once come to mind, this is still a vitally important approach to explore. Perhaps more than any other, it makes us question the social values that we place upon work (or "unleisure," as the ancient Greeks called it) as opposed to leisure, upon family as opposed to

---

* From *New Generation* (New York: National Committee on Employment of Youth), January 1964.

social responsibilities, upon the equality or inequality of income distribution, and upon the challenging possibilities inherent in automation and rising productivity.

But what kind of living standards can we achieve if we limit the number of people at work? How are we to decide who is to work and who is to be idle? Can we change our attitudes so much that we will favor more leisure over more goods? These are the questions that must be answered before we can decide whether this approach to the problem of unemployment makes any sense at all.

If, for the indefinite future, we were to limit the number of people at work to the present level of about 70 million, will the American economy be sufficiently productive to provide a decent standard of living for all of us? Happily, the answer to this question is affirmative, although it must be hedged with some interesting if possibly uncongenial qualifications.

At the present time, approximately 60 million consumer units—that is, families living together plus unattached individuals—share a total personal income well in excess of $400 billion a year. This means an average income per consumer unit of about $7,200.

While this is hardly enough for frequent trips to Europe, mink coats, or wall-to-wall carpeting, it is still sufficient to provide for all the basic necessities of life with something left over for savings and a few luxuries. After all, the average consuming unit today spends only 50 cents out of every dollar on food, clothing, housing, and household operation (much of which is on a luxurious level—the average American spends four times as much on food alone as the average Indian or Brazilian spends on everything), so that $3,000 or more is left over for payments on the car, gasoline, medical care, recreation, taxes, savings, and so on. Not affluent, but hardly in the poverty class.

Indeed, after allowing for the increased tax bite, the average family today is enjoying a full 50 percent more goods and services than in 1929 and one-third more than in 1947.

But what about the future? If 70 million workers today can provide our 60 million consumer units with an average income of $7,200, how well will they be able to provide for the approximately 72 million families and unattached individuals who will be on the scene 10 years from now?

Note that today the number of people at work exceeds the number of consumer units—in other words, most families have more than one breadwinner. But 10 years hence, the number of consumer units is likely to exceed 70 million, which means that we will then average fewer than one breadwinner per family if we hold the number of people at work to the present level of 70 million. Under these conditions, many more families than today would have no one going out to work; they will be retired or pursuing their education or just enjoying life.

Enjoying life, that is, if the 70 million people at work can, in fact, produce enough for everyone to maintain a decent standard of living. And here, too, the possibilities are on the hopeful side. If we can only keep up the rate of increase in output per man-hour that we have been able to achieve over the last 15 years, 70 million workers in 1973 will be sufficiently productive to give each consumer unit an average income of $7,900, in 1963 dollars.

This is an impressive fact: It underlines the dramatic potentials in automation and other forms of productivity improvement. It means that, *without employing one more person than we employ today,* we could produce enough in 1973 to provide all the new consumer units with annual incomes of $7,900, while giving each of the existing units (that are still in existence in 1973) a $700-a-year raise over present incomes.

Up to this point, however, we have been committing the statistical sin of talking in terms of averages. "Average" and "typical" are seldom synonymous. While the average family income in the United States at present is $7,200, two out of every three families have incomes *below* $7,200. For that two-thirds of our population, average income per consumer unit is only $4,700. The upper third of the income receivers, who take in altogether 60 percent of total family incomes, average the much higher figure of $11,000 a year.

The implication of these facts is clear. As long as so many Americans are forced to live at a level well below what most of us would consider comfortable, family breadwinners are going to feel under strong pressure to work and earn just as much as they possibly can. In other words, this utopian project of persuading people to withdraw from the labor force to enjoy leisure and education will find few takers until average family incomes move much higher or unless a massive redistribution of incomes can be achieved.

Here again the practical obstacles are clear. But here, too, the arithmetic is sufficiently intriguing to justify a brief look at the possibilities.

If, just for the moment, we accept the rather unrealistic assumption that *all* of the increase in incomes in the next 10 years would go only to those consumer units now earning less than $7,200 a year, we would be able to raise the average income of that group from $4,700 a year now to $6,300 a year by 1973, even with no more people at work than we have now (but, of course, assuming, as we did earlier, that output per man-hour continues rising at the postwar rate). In other words, $7,200 a year under these conditions becomes a theoretical possibility as a *minimum* rather than average family income. In short, poverty in the midst of plenty will become increasingly intolerable and irrational in our society.

Thus, disregarding for the moment the social and political forces that would surely impede the process, the ice-cold statistics do show that we have both the capacity and the ability to maintain adequate living standards in this country, even if we hold the number of people at work to the present level of 70 million. Fantastic as this idea may be in its *non*economic implications, it is nevertheless perfectly feasible from an economic viewpoint.[*]

But, of course, we would be foolish to ignore these social and political obstacles, for they are stubborn and real. Two of them are worth analysis here.

The first concerns the problem of distributing the fruits of our productive abundance. Since, by limiting the number of people at work, we also limit the supply of goods and services available for us to enjoy, an adequate standard of living for the lower-income groups depends unavoidably upon a major redistribution of incomes in their favor. And this is quite difficult to achieve, even if we thought it desirable to do so.

For example, under our present tax system, despite the complaints that one hears from upper-income-group taxpayers, we are actually accomplishing little or nothing in the way of income redistribution. The highest 20 percent of the income receivers take in 45 percent of total personal incomes before income taxes—and still have 44 percent of it after income taxes! Moreover, despite a sharp shift during

---

[*] Of course, we could enjoy far higher incomes than those discussed above if we expanded the number of jobs in line with the rise in the number of people of working age— even if we reduced the number of hours a year that each of us works. If the percentage of people of working age in the labor force holds at about the present level, and if productivity increases as it has since the war, we could have average family incomes of $9,000 a year or more by 1973.

the war and early postwar years, the share of this top 20 percent in total personal incomes after taxes has remained pretty stable over the past 10 years, even though the *absolute* dollar amounts earned by the lower-income groups have, of course, increased.

Furthermore, any determined effort to reduce the share of total income that accrues to the wealthy may have side effects so serious that we could all end up in worse condition than when we started. Most of the savings that make possible the expansion of American industry are concentrated among these upper-income groups. If we were to cut down their incomes or prevent them from rising, the flow of savings may be insufficient to provide the increased production needed to maintain or improve the living standards of everyone. The only alternative would be to force such an abnormally high level of saving on the lower-income groups that they would be able to buy very little more with their increased incomes. Finally, a flight of capital from the United States under these conditions would be a real possibility, with further, extremely serious consequences.

But it is not only the distribution of income that raises problems—the decision as to who is to work and who is to be idle (aside from the monetary rewards involved) is also difficult.

It would be complicated enough under any circumstances, but it is going to be especially complicated during the decade ahead. We are about to experience an unprecedentedly large and sudden change in the size and structure of our labor force; because of the surge of births after 1945, the number of people who would normally enter the labor force over the next 10 years will be twice that of the last 10 years.

Thus, while we started this discussion in terms of persuading about four million of our present population to give up working in favor of leisure, by 1973 we shall have to be using our arts of persuasion on about 14 million more! This will be especially difficult, for these young people are going to be eager to get married, have children, and set up their own households.

But would it be possible to persuade at least some of these young adults to postpone the day when they first go out to look for a job? And, to the extent that we are unable to find all of our 14 million recruits for leisure from this group, can we look perhaps to the older workers, say, those between 55 and 64 years old? And what about the middle-aged women who have flocked into the labor force in such large numbers in recent years—can we persuade some of them to stay home or perhaps to resume their education?

The possibilities here are truly intriguing. If we project current labor-force participation rates 10 years ahead, about 19 million young people in the 15 to 24 age group will be working or seeking work in 1973, along with 11 million older men and women in the 55 to 64 age group and 11 million women in the 35 to 54 group.

If 14 million out of these 41 million people in the crucial age groups were to withdraw from (or refrain from entering) the labor force, any number of exciting possibilities present themselves. For example:

Just about everybody who wanted to go to college could do so. We could arrange our lives so that people who wanted to could retire at 55, instead of waiting until they reach 65. Middle-aged women could give up working to engage in community activities, spend more time with their children, take up volunteer teaching activities (which we shall need in large quantities), pursue their own education, and so on.

In each case, of course, we are implying that the family involved will have less income than it might otherwise have. Yet, we have already seen that the American economy will be sufficiently productive by 1973 so that no family, in theory at least, need live in poverty even though fewer members of the family go out to work.

What this question really turns on, then, is our society's fundamental attitudes toward work as contrasted with the uses of leisure. Clearly everybody would rather work than starve. Most people would rather work than live at a subsistence level. But, when we reach the not-quite-but-almost-affluent status of American families, the choice between what an additional dollar's income might buy and what an additional hour of leisure can provide becomes more difficult.

In short, as our productivity rises, we shall be in a position to question increasingly the values that our past way of life has generated. How badly, for example, will we need *more* appliances, *more* convenience packed into our food, *more* automobiles in the family, *more* new dresses for every social season? To the extent that we choose to do without some of these things, the urgency to raise our incomes will be dampened. We shall, in other words, begin to value the uses of leisure more highly than we value the extra things that a dollar's worth of additional income might buy.

If we do shift our values in these directions, then we shall also favor the choice of *voluntary* unemployment in the form of more years of education, earlier retirement, and so on. Then these withdrawals from the labor force can open up more room for the new workers who will be seeking jobs and who might otherwise be involuntarily unemployed. The attractive possibility here is not just in the arithmetic, not just in the statistical fact that voluntary unemployment can replace involuntary unemployment— rather it is in the tangible realization that our fabulously productive American economy can now permit life to be lived rather than slaved away.

Because it implies a profound upheaval in our social values and standards of success, this is probably the most revolutionary of all the varied suggestions for the elimination of unemployment. No one even knows how to sell the idea to the American people—we can hardly merchandise more years of college, more hours sitting in the sunshine, more reading and music and art in the same way that we merchandise the jumbo automobile, sudsier suds, and foamier beer.

But what a deliciously utopian idea it is: Perhaps someday idleness will be so desirable in America that we will be unable to find even 70 million people to do our nation's work!

CAN BUSINESS GRASP THE FUTURE?*

Few people would argue with the proposition that achievement of certain widely desired national goals—adjustment to disarmament, maintenance of high employment, eradication of poverty, and pursuit of domestic tranquillity—would be extremely difficult without a dynamic business environment. But what is not so generally recognized is that there may be fundamental conflicts here between means and ends, between the adjustments required to meet these national goals and an environment that would be compatible with prosperous and venturesome business firms.

To put the matter in terms of a cliché: If what is good for business is good for the nation, does it follow that what is good for the nation is good for business? And if not, can we achieve the national goals we seek in the absence of high business morale?

---

* From the *Nation*, January 13, 1964.

Nearly 30 years ago, John Maynard Keynes had this to say on the subject:

> If animal spirits are dimmed and spontaneous optimism falters, leaving us to depend on nothing but a mathematical expectation, enterprise will fade and die. . . . This means that economic prosperity is excessively dependent upon a political and social atmosphere which is congenial to the average businessman.

The essential question, then, is whether the political and social atmosphere we seek is going to be sufficiently congenial to the average businessman to assure us of the "animal spirits" and "spontaneous optimism" without which "enterprise will fade and die."

Here, roughly in order of importance, are the dilemmas that I hope we can successfully resolve in the years ahead:

Goal 1: Peace and disarmament. But can we adjust to disarmament without substituting, at least in part, *non*-defense government expenditures for defense expenditures?

Goal 2: High employment and the elimination of poverty. But to achieve this goal in the face of any unprecedented increase in the number of people seeking jobs, can the demand for goods and services in this country grow at least 20 percent faster than in the extraordinarily prosperous decade 1947–1957, and 60 percent faster than during the past five years?

Goal 3: Eradication of racial discrimination and all conflict based on race, color, or creed. But can we provide full constitutional economic rights to all our citizens unless the business community recognizes its essential role in this process?

Goal 4: Full use of the potentials inherent in an economy of abundance. But can we benefit from these blessings before they drown us in involuntary unemployment?

Goal 5: Attainment of what John Kenneth Galbraith calls "social balance"—the proper allocation of our output and income between public and private goods. Yet, despite the desperate need for more goods and services of a community nature, businessmen are not alone in resisting and resenting the so-called burdens that support the public sector.

If these are our goals, will businessmen accept the adjustments essential for their achievement?

The first factor that inhibits full business contribution to national goals is something over which businessmen, whether they approve of it or deplore it, have really very little control. Ever since 1929, but most evidently since 1941, the nation's decision-making power has been shifting away from the businessman and corporate manager and toward the government, the scientist, and the university.

The communication links between business and these other groups are tenuous at best and are complicated by fundamentally different attitudes toward monetary rewards, privilege, and property. It is no wonder that the business community feels increasingly isolated and frustrated in relation to the mainstream of events. No longer completely the master of his own fate, far less master of the fate of others, the businessman must face a world whose main problems are neither made by business nor soluble by business.

This leads us to the second source of conflict between our national goals and a dynamic business environment—the pressure for social change. For times of rapid social change, of restlessness and impatience among the impoverished and underprivileged, are times when business confidence is disturbed and "animal spirits" are dimmed. I do not want to imply that businessmen as a class are opposed to social change, or that they oppose it more stubbornly than many other groups in our society. On the contrary, many businessmen as individuals and many business organizations are working hard to improve their communities and the welfare of their employees.

The question at issue is not the receptivity of businessmen to social change as such. Rather, it is the willingness of businessmen to be dynamic in their *businesses*—to invest, expand, and innovate—in a time of intensified social restlessness that brings with it antibusiness philosophies and cries of "Share the wealth."

This brings us to the third and perhaps most important block in the way of full contribution from business to the achievement of these goals. That block is the government. Since government is the primary engine for effecting social change in our system, the bitter distrust of businessmen toward it, and in particular toward the size of its budget, is a symptom of our malaise.

It is part of the American tradition that the relationship between business and government should be bad: The most casual student of our history can cite numerous instances. In the most recent past, the fracas between President Kennedy and Roger Blough was a dramatic if unpleasant reminder that the tradition persists. As Professor Mason of Harvard pointed out not long ago, European businessmen can say, "Some of my best friends are civil servants," and really mean it; but almost the only civil servants an American businessman would accept as friends are other businessmen on temporary loan to the government.

There have been times when we could afford the luxury of this traditional bitterness, and other times when we could not. Surely the agony of the Depression was prolonged by the malevolence that was clung to by leaders on both sides. And the years ahead, immediately and perhaps for decades, will be a poor time for feuding between business and political leaders.

We need a prosperous economy to achieve our national goals, but we will be unable to achieve those goals—including a prosperous economy—without governmental leadership and assistance. To repeat, can we really expect the demands of industry and consumers to grow 60 percent faster in the next eight to ten years than they grew during the explosively prosperous decade of 1947–1957? But if we are unable to achieve this extraordinary rate of growth, except perhaps for very short periods, then we must be willing to see the government's share of the gross national product expand beyond its present level of about 20 percent. Only thus will total demand expand fast enough to make it profitable for businessmen to produce at full capacity and to employ everyone who seeks a job. And, in the light of these same calculations, is it reasonable to assume that we could adjust to a major reduction in defense spending unless it were rapidly offset by government support in other areas?

To go further: Would the barriers against the Negroes have been reduced as far as they have without the intervention of the courts and the Department of Justice? Can we solve the problems of abundance without giving more thought to the structure of income and wealth distribution in this country? Can business alone satisfy the terrifyingly impatient demands of the underdeveloped lands for higher living standards? Is it proper to think of fattening our national living standards while our educational and medical facilities are inadequate, our cities an aesthetic and social disgrace, our civil servants underpaid, our police forces undermanned, our few remaining open recreational areas overcrowded beyond belief or gobbled up by commercial enterprise?

But this raises a further disturbing possibility. If the American businessman today sees a world of social ferment, feels increasingly isolated from the centers of strategic decision-making, and fears the growing size of governmental budgets, he is likely to develop an uncertainty, timidity, and defensiveness, which in the end would make it impossible for us to achieve the goals we seek within the framework of our present order. Then, if the American people are determined to achieve these goals, the present order might have to yield to the goals, rather than the goals yielding to the order.

At this point we should be honest with ourselves: Ours is not the only method the world has found to make progress. We may see much that is repugnant in the means that other peoples have selected for roughly similar ends, but we can no longer lightheartedly insist that these other systems are bound to fail, whereas we shall certainly succeed.

For example, will the Soviet economy have more difficulty than we in adjusting to disarmament and a liquidation of the cold war? Is their rate of economic growth any slower than ours? Racial tensions exist in the USSR, but are they any more intense or any less capable of solution than ours? Have the Russians given a lower priority than we to education, urban renewal, the pursuit of scientific truth, public recreation, medical care, or the arts?

Here is the real challenge to the business community, still the keystone of what we call the "present order." The Marxists know it well. They no longer preach that capitalism must topple from its own weight, that it inexorably leads to increasing misery and thus inevitably to revolution. Today they understand that capitalism can save itself—primarily through the demand stimuli that government can create. But now we face the serious danger that the capitalists themselves will bring on their own ruin by stubbornly resisting the very policies that can be their salvation.

Our major obstacles, then, arise not so much from the maladjustments inherent in the free-enterprise system, nor from the difficulty of the adjustments required to achieve our national goals. Rather, they are produced by the impact of these adjustments on the animal spirits and spontaneous optimism of business leaders, on the venturesomeness and dynamic qualities that are essential for our success.

We shall be unable to achieve our goals within our present order unless we enjoy a high and rising level of business activity; that, in turn, depends upon the businessman's acceptance of deep-seated changes in the modern world and modern society, not all of which may be congenial to him. The overwhelmingly important fact that he must face is that his choices are limited. For failure to achieve the goals of peace, full employment, and social progress within our present framework may result in an entirely new environment about whose lack of congeniality he can have no possible doubt.

THE EVIL CONGLOMERATE: MYTH OR REALITY?[*]

In the halls of Congress, at the highest levels of the Administration and in the groves of academe, high-minded men are now mounting a powerful offensive against conglomerate companies. These companies, and the brash, unorthodox businessmen who lead them, are being accused of destroying competition, of deceiving innocent stockholders through the issuance of funny money, and of threatening the very foundations of our capitalist system.

The offensive has been accompanied by such a deafening bombardment and has been set in such altruistic terms that the defense has seemed disturbingly weak and inarticulate. But a strong positive case is there to be made in favor of the conglomerates, and it is high time someone picked up the cudgels and went into battle in their defense.

Mr. McLaren, Chief of the Antitrust Division of the Justice Department, is basing his attack mainly on Section 7 of the Clayton Act, which prohibits one company's acquisition of another company's stock when, among other things, the effect of such acquisition may be "to restrain such commerce in any section of the community or tend to create a monopoly in any line of commerce." Thus, for example,

---

[*] A Bernstein-Macaulay bulletin, June 1, 1969.

Ling-Tamco-Vought (LTV) may not acquire Jones and Laughlin Steel because, if LTV really wants to go into the steel business, they should build a new steel company and promote competition in that fashion. But this assumes, of course, that LTV would in fact have built new steel plants of their own if entry into the industry through the acquisition route were blocked—a highly questionable assumption.

In contrast to mergers between companies producing similar goods for similar markets or between companies with a supplier-customer relationship, conglomerate mergers would seem to have no *inherent* tendency to restrain competition or to create monopolies. Indeed, in many cases, a conglomerate consisting of strong and weak elements can divert resources from the stronger elements to the weaker, thereby in all likelihood preserving and enhancing competition in the markets in which the weaker company is operating. J & L, for example, operates in an industry where U.S. Steel and Bethlehem account for nearly 40 percent of the market and the next four companies take only 26 percent. Can strengthening J & L weaken competition in steel?

Of course, the larger a company is, the greater the potential market power it can wield. Conglomerate mergers also create possibilities for reciprocal buying and other forms of hidden price discrimination. However, to attack conglomerates on this basis is to defy the fundamental principles of the system of law under which we live. Under this system, we are subject to prosecution for *acts*, not for capability. Many of us are capable of committing evil acts and most of us at one time or another have even contemplated them. But the law should protect us from prosecution until we actually go out and try to perform some illegal action.

If a conglomerate company, or any other company, acts to restrain trade, fix prices, discriminate among customers, or act in any other way contrary to law, it should be prosecuted immediately. The mere capability of such actions, however, seems to be a questionable basis for preventing the merger from taking place.

Most conglomerate companies in recent years have acquired other companies by issuing securities rather than by paying in cash. The hope and expectation is that the earning power of the acquired company will be more than sufficient to maintain the service required by the new securities.

Although the patterns vary widely and the ingeniousness of some of the security packages occasionally defies imagination, most payments have included straight debt, convertible bonds or preferreds, warrants, and common stock. In general, the objective has been to postpone the ultimate dilution of equity interest in the acquiring company for as long a period as possible and, through the device of warrants, to avoid any interest or dividend payments whatsoever as part of the payment price.

However—and this is a crucially important point—the common stockholder of the acquired company has in every case received a package of securities that (1) has given him a larger current income than he was receiving formerly, (2) has had a market value in excess of the market value of his common stock prior to the initiation of the transaction, and (3) has involved, at least in part, the issuance of securities senior to the common stock. He has, as a result, hardly come out with anything much to complain about: He has had something of a windfall in capital values and income, and has come out with a preferred security position besides.

Now, it is of course perfectly possible that the management of the conglomerate company will make a mess of things at some point in the future. They may pass dividends, default on debts, and render warrants worthless. Again, however, the conglomerate as such has no *inherent* tendencies toward bankruptcy; bankruptcy has occurred in more respectable quarters over the years. Furthermore, the stockholder of the acquired company is under absolutely no obligation to accept or retain the new securities issued to him by the conglomerate—he can go out into the market and sell them anytime he pleases. If he ends up stuck in a rotten deal, he has no one to blame but himself, for the balance sheets and income statements of the conglomerates are there to be studied with just as much care as the statements of AT&T or General Motors.

Furthermore, before we weep for the poor stockholder of the acquired company as he stuffs this supposedly worthless paper into his safe-deposit box, let us shed a more genuine tear for the stockholder of the company whose management is underutilizing its assets, missing opportunities for growth, and limiting dividend payouts while needlessly accumulating cash or making investments at continuously declining rates of return.

This last point is crucial to the entire argument. The difficulties our economic system faces do not lie in the aggressiveness of the managers of the conglomerates. Rather, it is to be found in the large number of companies, including some of the giants of American industry, who sit like fat cats on billions of dollars of assets earning far less than they could earn under more inspired management. While this is hardly against the law in any strictly legal sense, it flies right in the face of the basic principles under which our system operates, namely, that capital should move to those areas where the rate of return is the highest.

Nearly 30 years ago, in a landmark book entitled *The Modern Corporation and Private Property*, Adolph Berle and Gardiner Means drew our attention to the disturbing implications of the separation of ownership and control brought about by the development of the modern corporation. As a result of the enormous dispersion of corporate ownership and the ease with which the stockholder can sell his interest in any corporation, owners have come to exercise less and less control over management. Consequently, management has become self-perpetuating. Internal corporate politics rather than objectives of maximum profitability have become the determinant for advancement in many companies. Immune from overthrow, unimaginative managements have presided for decades over many companies while more creative competitors have left them far behind.

The conglomerates provide a direct confrontation to the senility of American industry on two counts.

First, through the tender offer and takeover bids, mistakenly frowned upon by so many, ownership suddenly has a meaningful method for voting for or against management. No matter how small management's ownership interest may be, a well-run company need have no fears on this score; no matter how widely dispersed corporate ownership may be, no bad management can escape the consequences of the mobilization of ownership made possible through the takeover bid. Under our free-enterprise system, the race is supposed to be to the swiftest; the new aggressive techniques of the conglomerates assure us that no one will feel comfortable lagging behind the parade.

Second, and equally important, the conglomerates emphasize another fundamental principle of our economics: The name of the game is not steel, autos, electricity, or plywood—*it is profits*. Too many managements for too many years have plowed back too much money into making the same old product at ever lower rates of return, simply because that is what they always made. The conglomerate manager says, "I have X amounts of resources to be deployed; I do not care where I deploy them, so long as I can maximize my rate of return on those resources."

This is hardly the stuff that stifles competition or destroys capitalism. On the contrary, it represents the essence of the revitalization that much of our hidebound industry so badly needs.

IS GOLD THE ONLY THING THAT'S KEEPING US HONEST?*

Columbus once observed that gold was such wonderful stuff that it could even get you into Heaven. While it has perhaps lost some of this luster with the passage of centuries as sophistication has grown among men who deal in monetary matters, a good many people still believe that our links to gold are the only solid obstacles that keep us from going right to Hell.

The role of gold, not only in our monetary structure, but in our minds and hearts as well, is crucial to every investment decision, for the degree of liquidity that exists throughout the capital markets of the world obviously has a great deal to do with the level of security prices. The future trend of bonds and stocks will be profoundly influenced by our decisions to worship gold or to abolish its worship, to change its price or to hold it constant, and to tie our currencies to it more tightly or less.

The orthodox view of gold, although now somewhat on the defensive, nevertheless still has powerful supporters. The

_____

* From *Institutional Investor*, November 1967.

new Special Drawing Rights created by the International Monetary Fund (IMF) are basically tied to gold. Indeed, the thorniest problem in the negotiations leading to the creation of a new international currency is related to the character and rigidity of these links to gold. The adherents of this position find the only true value in gold and fear the recklessness of men freed from the discipline it imposes on their actions.

A contrary view of gold would take the position that gold is valueless, useless, and obsolete. One could go further and argue that those who pin their hopes for the future on gold are unreasonable and are pursuing a course that is positively dangerous.

I can support this position only by making some statements that may be startling and others that I know full well are overstatements of the case. Unfortunately, this seems unavoidable. Our responses to questions involving gold are terribly cluttered by emotional and visceral reactions, by the myths and distortions of history, and by the persistent propaganda emitted by those whose vested interests are intimately tied up with it. Only statements of the strongest sort can penetrate the barriers we all erect to a rational view of the subject.

Of course, emotional responses to the subject of gold are by no means a modern phenomenon. One of the most famous—and one of the most significant—temper tantrums in history occurred when Moses, returning from his dialogue with God on Mount Sinai, found the Jews worshipping a golden calf. Here he was, bringing to his people from the Almighty a code of human relationships that rested upon a fundamental belief in the ability of men to live with one another in peace and mutual respect, and what does he find? He finds the Jews in an act of incredible irrationality—the frenzied worship of an object of no value and no meaning. No wonder he smashed the tablets to bits!

Time has done little to diminish the meaning of this story. It represents the unbridgeable gap between those who believe that men are capable of taking care of themselves in a reasonable manner and those who have no faith in that ability. This is really what the controversy over gold is all about, and it is therefore the core of my argument.

But the story about Moses and the golden calf is not the only one relevant to our discussion. Take King Midas. Since everything he touched turned to gold, he became a very poor man instead of a wealthy one. He had no clothes he could wear or food he could eat. His house was so heavy and ductile that it collapsed. He could no longer turn the pages of his books or wield his sword for defense. The moral of this story is that gold may be a beautiful object of adornment, but beyond that it has no intrinsic value at all. The more of it we accumulate, the less we have of the things that give real meaning to wealth.

General de Gaulle might well remember this fable, for while the French have taken a good deal of gold away from us in recent years, we have consumed much delicious food, drunk many bottles of fabulous wine, and titillated ourselves with haunting perfumes in the process—to say nothing of the enormously profitable and productive French assets that the gold has brought us. Who in the end is better off as a result of this exchange, the French or we?

If, then, the value of gold is symbolic rather than real, we must nevertheless recognize that it has certain unique physical attributes that enable it to carry out its historic role so effectively. Extraordinarily resistant to oxygen, it never tarnishes or deteriorates. Extremely high in density, it packs a large weight into a small space. Scarce and increasing in supply much more slowly than the growth of the world economy, it seems always to be in demand. All of these features make it a highly efficient form of money and go far to explain the curious activity of men in digging it up out of the ground only in order to bury it back again.

Now note that, with the price fixed, the output of gold each year is determined primarily by the grade of ore in the mines and by the productivity of the men and equipment working those mines. In other words, the rate of gold output throughout the world is dependent upon physical relationships and upon the business decisions of mine managers rather than upon the decisions of the central bankers and finance ministers of the community of nations.

To those who adhere to a belief in the superiority of the gold standard, this separation of authority is crucial. If the central bankers and finance ministers have no participation in the decisions determining the base to which the overall supply of money is tied, then, in effect, they are unable to increase the supply of money beyond rigidly set limits, no matter how much they may want to do so and no matter how compelling they believe their reasons to be.

Parenthetically, I might mention the well-known tendency of central bankers and finance ministers to abandon the tie to gold when they have felt the need for larger increases in the money supply to be compelling, even though that is precisely what is not supposed to happen.

Now, all of this has a great deal to do with the Ten Commandments and the golden calf. Those who, like Moses, believe that men not only can but should manage their affairs in a reasonable and rational manner will align themselves against the gold standard and everything it signifies. Those who, on the other hand, doubt the ability of men to be wise in their deliberations will want to leave the ultimate decision as to the supply of our purchasing power to nature and other forces over which we have no control. In short, much of what you feel about gold will be determined by your basic philosophical and ethical view of man and his role on earth.

But the cleavage between the opponents and adherents of gold is more than just philosophical: It is political as well. This is suggested in what I have just said. If the monetary authorities are limited in the amount of money they can create, and if the gold base expands at only a modest rate, then the expansion of the economy is likely to be slower than it might have been otherwise. We know that spending and production can expand faster than the money supply under certain conditions and for limited periods of time, but we also know, as the experience of 1966 dramatically demonstrated, that the money barrier will ultimately halt and then reverse the economy's growth.

Thus, to the extent that gold sets upper limits to the money supply, it prevents an economy from attempting too much at once, from moving into an inflationary spiral, from overextending its credit and financial institutions. This is all to the good, of course. But it can also fatally slow progress. In a deflationary atmosphere, businessmen are timorous rather than enterprising, cautious rather than bold, and expansion and change in the economy slow down rather than move ahead. A dynamic business environment and a willingness to undertake social experiment and reform are possible only in an expansionary atmosphere.

In short, the cleavage of the viewpoints on gold is symptomatic of the age-old struggle between the progressive and the conservative, in the fullest meanings of those words—of the differences between those in a hurry to get things done and those who want to slow down. Ask a man how he feels about gold and you will soon know a good deal about his entire attitude toward society.

The most extreme example of this, of course, was Lenin, who predicted that one day the Soviets would line their public conveniences with gold. But it was no coincidence that William Jennings Bryan despised the limitations on economic progress implied in the establishment of the gold standard and therefore railed against the crucifixion of mankind "on a cross of gold," or that John Maynard Keynes expressed his skepticism of the gold standard in his earliest writings and was the architect of a new world monetary system to liberate us from gold. At the other extreme, we might point to a man like Franz Pick, whose utter cynicism about the morality of governments and men has led him for years to predict financial disasters that have never materialized. Economists like Henry Hazlett and Walter Spahr combine a highly critical viewpoint of monetary management with extremely conservative political philosophies.

Finally, this use of gold as a focal point for fundamental political differences is dramatized by the confrontation between the French and ourselves over international monetary reform. The French are using the gold as a lever to slow down what they believe is our haste to buy up or blow up most of the world's assets. More profoundly, perhaps, the traditional and unshakable French desire to hoard gold relates to the history of a people whose rulers have seldom been notably wise and unvenal.

All of this should make my own position clear. While obviously we must try to avoid the kind of overextension and overspending that would lead to an uncontrollable inflationary spiral, American history lends impressive evidence to support the belief that we can handle our affairs well enough without the hindrances and complications of a mechanical and arbitrary barrier to the achievement of our objectives.

This leads us, then, to some discussion of the odd notion that we can break down these barriers and still have the best of all possible worlds if we will only raise the price of gold by a substantial sum—say, by doubling it to $70 an ounce. The proponents of this move argue that it would increase the world's liquidity a lot faster than the plans currently under way at the IMF, in that it would enable each ounce of monetary gold now existing to buy twice as much as it did before, and, at the same time, it would encourage a much higher level of new gold production. Indeed, they go on to say, the poor gold miners have had no increase in the price of their product for nearly 35 years, during which time the average price of most other products has just about tripled in the United States and gone up a lot more in the rest of the world.

This last point is worth discussing first, because we are frequently called upon to feel sorry for an industry whose selling price has been frozen for such a long period of widespread inflation. But let us go back in time to 1933, when gold was $20.67 an ounce. At that time, the wholesale-price index had fallen by about 30 percent from the 1929 level and was more than 50 percent below its post–World War I peak, reached in 1920. But the price of gold had not fallen by one penny. Furthermore, when really useful commodities like wheat or copper or lumber or coffee were going begging without any buyers, the gold miners were assured of a market for everything they could produce at the going price. And at that moment, by a stroke of President Roosevelt's wand, they were assured of a market for everything they could produce at a price nearly double $20.67 an ounce! As against 1900, when we went on the gold standard at $20.67, the wholesale commodity price was up only 20 percent—and lower than it was in 1910—while the price of gold was raised 60 percent. In my opinion, the gold miners will be working off that particular windfall for a long time to come.

Furthermore, recent data indicate that the South African gold mines, which produce more than three-quarters of the free world's gold, are not having too bad a time of it. Their production is currently running more than 40 percent above the 1960 level. Their cost per ton has risen less than 5 percent over this period: By mining richer veins, they have held their profit per ton to within 2 percent of where it was six or seven years ago. Their profit margin runs about 50 percent on a commodity that has always been in a seller's market.

From the strict business view of gold mining, therefore, the case for a higher price is difficult to support. And this ignores the disastrous consequences of a price increase to the mutual confidence and trust on which all of our current monetary arrangements rest, not the least of which would be the windfall profit to those, like the French, who hastened to flee from the dollar rather than stand by us.

In any case, why should we take steps to encourage and stimulate the production of a commodity so utterly useless when our own country lacks the goods and services we need for a decent quality of life for all and when two-thirds of the world's population live in an abysmal state of poverty? In World War II we had the good sense to shut down the gold mines, because we could not afford to waste labor and resources when we needed them in the much more important business of destroying the Nazis and the Japanese. Today, while hunger, disease, and slums remain as even more intractable enemies to a peaceful and rational world, should we take opposite steps and divert more labor and resources to the useless business of digging gold out of the ground?

How irrational can we be? Today the South Africans earn more than a billion dollars a year digging this useless stuff out of the ground and selling it to us so that we can stick it back underground once again. This is what is known as sound finance. Would we be more irrational if we gave the South Africans a billion dollars a year and asked them to provide useful goods and services that would improve the living standards of the shockingly poor continent on which they live? We are out a billion dollars either way, and the South Africans earn a billion dollars either way, but one way all we have is some useless stuff underground, while the other can help lead to a more stable and prosperous world.

But this leads me to conclude by some conjecture on an intriguing possibility suggested by this discussion.

As we can see, uselessness is an essential characteristic of money. If something is useful, we cannot afford to hoard it indefinitely in antiseptic vaults many feet below the earth or even to pass it indefinitely from hand to hand. For example, we could never smoke the cigarettes we used as money in Germany after the last war, because then they would be smoked up instead of continuing their existence as a means of payment. Similarly, while people have used many different valuable objects or commodities as money in the history of the world, they ultimately had to resort to symbols of those useful objects, in the form of coin or paper notes, because they needed the objects themselves to fulfill the needs of their daily lives.

In our own time, paper money costs very little indeed to produce, while our primary form of money—bank deposits—requires no more than a punch on a bookkeeping machine or electronic calculator to come into existence or to be transferred from one holder to another. Gold is particularly anachronistic, therefore, because it is extremely costly to produce—the cost of labor and resources it absorbs annually would be sufficient to pay for the production of about 100,000 dwelling units a year.

Hence, a modern and sophisticated world should adopt one or the other of two possible solutions to this problem. On the one hand, we can completely abandon the production of something so completely useless. On the other hand—and this would be a much happier solution—perhaps we can find a real use for gold.

I understand, for example, that its resistance to heat has led to certain applications in our space program. Perhaps similar applications exist. A rapid expansion of useful outlets for gold would be wonderful, even if it results in some increase in the price.

I say that it would be wonderful, because—as we have just seen in the case of silver—it would lead to the demonetization of gold without any panic, without any sense that we were demoralizing our currency, without any fussing or argument about myths and shibboleths that stand in the way of rational solutions. As we eliminated cattle and beads and women and silver as forms of currency in the past, simply because we had more useful things to do with them, so we should welcome an opportunity to do away with gold as money because we have some better use to which to put it.

A MODEST PROPOSAL*

Recently a small group of policy makers from Washington met with several respected Wall Streeters in order to discuss the problem of how to finance the government in face of the general unpopularity of bonds without either impeding the progress of the recovery or feeding the generally expected inflation.

---

*With apologies to Jonathan Swift. A Bernstein-Macaulay bulletin, September 1, 1958, written by Linhart Stearns.

The professional economists and experts on banking and government finance did not come up with new ideas that met with any general enthusiasm. The meeting seemed destined to run into a dead end when a Mr. X made a startling proposal.

Mr. X attacked the problem from an entirely fresh point of view. He said that, as he was a partner in a large stock-exchange firm, he was closer to the thinking of the public than were the rest of the group. It was only because of this more common touch that he dared to speak up among such an erudite and responsible meeting of fiscal experts. But as securities and their marketing were his business, and as government bonds were securities that had to be sold just like other issues, he felt that he might be able to contribute a plan.

Mr. X pointed out that the public would not buy bonds because of the conviction that the inflation was inexorable and that the holder of bonds was bound to lose out in purchasing power. Besides, almost everybody already had suffered losses in bonds, and it is well known that people are loath to buy securities in which they once lost money. Therefore, anything called a "bond" had become an almost unsalable item unless it contained features so favorable as to be ruinous to the issuer.

On the other hand, the public's eagerness to buy anything that was called a "common stock" seemed limitless, and little discretion was brought to bear in making the decisions of what to buy and how much to pay.

In the circumstances, Mr. X thought that if the government did what any intelligent underwriting house would do, namely, tailor its issues to the desires of the market, there should be good promise of a successful flotation. Obviously the government should attune itself to the times—bonds were passé, stocks were now the thing, and, therefore, the government should bring out a common-stock issue.

Calling a government issue a "stock" rather than a "bond" would in itself assure its acceptance by the public. But Mr. X thought that the success of the issue could be further assured if it capitalized on the investing public's enthusiasms and if it were given a certain aura in the market. As regards the latter, of course, there were limits to the advertising and promotion either printed or spoken. It was important not to run afoul of the Securities and Exchange Commission (SEC) or the various state security commissions. However, the market itself was eager to emphasize the favorable aspects of any common-stock issue and, in fact, was prone to imagine favorable factors without any unethical encouragement. Thus, Mr. X pointed out, a common-stock prospectus could be circumspect and straightforward in its statements and still assure the issue a good reception. In fact, in several instances common-stock issues had gone over with a bang merely because his firm had headed the selling group—nobody seemed to care what was in the prospectus.

Mr. X felt that the government was in the position to issue the perfect common stock, which couldn't fail to gain the ultimate in popularity. Investors looked for certain things in common stocks. These were (1) growth, (2) protection against inflation, (3) market popularity, (4) leverage. Contrary to old-fashioned opinion, investors were hardly interested in cash dividends or rate of income return or book values. They even gave little heed to price because of the general conviction that any price paid for a stock today would be proved low in the future—growth, inflation, and market popularity would make any caviling about value superfluous.

Now, the government stock issue could be designed to satisfy all four investor objectives. To this end Mr. X proposed that 3 percent of all government *expenditures* accrue as earnings for the government's common stock. It was too early to discuss the technical details, but in general each department would have to pay three cents into the common-stock fund for every dollar it spent. (This would not be too hard for the bureaucrats to swallow because sales taxes were already unbiquitous. Besides, it might be a good thing if this 3 percent tax on government spending served to remind officials of the nuisances and burdens the rest of us bear.)

The prospectus of the issue could carry a table showing the course of government *expenditures*, say, from 1929 to date as well as the corresponding figures for 3 percent thereof. It would be obvious that the earnings for the common stock would have grown more than twentyfold in the three decades. Few blue chips now outstanding could equal this growth record. The public judges growth by the record of the past and extends that record into the distant future. There is no doubt that, in view of the public's confidence in the future, it would envisage a truly startling earning prospect for the government's common stock. It would probably be considered the premier growth stock in the country.

The stock would also be considered a perfect inflation hedge. Its earnings would be geared exactly to the one factor the public believes determines the extent of inflation—government spending. Furthermore, the stock would represent ownership in a huge amount of material things both above and below ground, to say nothing of things in the air and, perhaps in the near future, on other planets. The real estate in Washington alone is a tremendous inflation hedge. Then, there are millions of acres of public lands, national parks, military installations, and so on. The public would not be backward in conjecturing that oil, uranium, or any number of other riches would be found and prove to make the stock even a better inflation hedge. Mr. X reminded his audience that it was not necessary for the investing public to believe that any of these assets would ever be sold at a profit or distributed. Stocks were considered inflation hedges if the public knew or guessed that assets existed even if they were never to be realized on.

Market popularity for the issue was assured by its size and the huge operations of the venture. No other issue could possibly be kept in the public eye so much as the government's common stock. Every day hundreds of items about some aspect of the issuer's operations would be prominently displayed in the press and reported over the air. News about an issuer keeps investors interested in the issuer's stock and the government stock would enjoy the highest amount of advertising. Mr. X said that in this connection there was only one drawback—the management of the venture might not be highly regarded, and there would be some doubts about the enterprise's efficiency. Such reservations, however, would not react too badly on the stock because poor management and inefficiency would increase government expenditures and thus would increase the stock's earning power!

With respect to leverage, the stock would also appeal to the public. It might follow over $280 *billion* of debt and many billions of contingent liabilities. Mr. X felt that probably the stock would at most represent an equity of 40 percent. This would depend on the issue price, which he discussed later.

As the stock was to be presented as a growth security, it was important to keep the cash dividend extremely low but to raise it consistently by minute amounts. A generous dividend would give the stock the wrong aura for it then would be considered a good income stock suitable for widows and orphans and not a dynamic security. Everybody knows that sound, good income-bearing stocks are not too popular. Present-day investors don't want income but only a capital gain. It would be a great mistake to make the dividend too attractive.

Mr. X made an estimate of the probable price at which the stock could be issued. So ideal an issue should command a price/earnings ratio at least as high as those that have been applied to such stocks as IBM, 3M, Polaroid, and so on. These have at times sold at about 45 times earnings, and Mr. X said that his firm would surely be willing to issue the government's stock on this basis. Perhaps they might even be willing to exceed this figure. On the basis of government expenditures of $80 billion, the earnings applicable to the stock would be $2.4 billion. Multiplying this figure by 45 would bring the total value of the issue to $108 billion. He suggested a price of $400 a share (around the price of IBM), which means that 270 million shares would be issued—about as many shares as General Motors has outstanding.

Mr. X pointed out that, if it were desirable to issue more stock, increasing the percentage of expenditures reserved for the stock could offset any dilution. He mentioned, also, that warrants to buy the stock—say at 20 percent above issue price—could be sold to satisfy the most speculatively inclined investors and to bring additional sums into the Treasury. At a later date convertible-bond issues would also be possible.

Mr. X's idea was considered so novel that none of those at the meeting was willing to support him except behind closed doors. However, it was deemed advisable to get the public reaction to the plan and that, therefore, its outlines should be "leaked off the record" as a trial balloon. This is why this was written.

AN IMMODEST PROPOSAL*

Our readers of long standing may recall that from time to time we have reported on the deliberations of a small group of tough-minded and creative business executives and university people who meet occasionally to advise the government in a highly confidential way on some of the major issues of the day.

We recently had the opportunity to see the minutes of a meeting held by this group in early 1964. The discussion was fascinating in its own right, but, with the advantages of hindsight, we found it even more remarkable.

The group had been asked to consider how the United States might find some way to improve its steadily deteriorating reputation for progressiveness, compassion, and generosity. The most interesting part of the meeting began with the statement of a man who had just returned from an extended trip to the country of Bwongwham, a crowded, underdeveloped country, but one in which most of the upper-class people, the religious leaders, and the military had had European educations. The country had

_____
* A Bernstein–Macaulay bulletin, June 1, 1967.

been divided into two separate nations, however, known as North Bwongwham and South Bwongwham.

"Let us try one really massive foreign-aid program," suggested our friend. "Let us give this nation of 35 million people about $20 billion a year in real aid. This will build their roads and schools and power plants, set up their port facilities, establish a proper transportation system, and equip their farms with machinery and fertilizer. Let us at the same time send 400,000 or 500,000 young Americans over there to show them how to do it, to guide their planning, to help with everything from ditch-digging to the use of computers.

"After three or four years of this, we will have a real showcase, particularly if we are just as generous to the less friendly North Bwongwhamians as we are to the Southerners. Incidentally, the Bwongwhamian Communist party is still relatively independent of Russian and Chinese influence, which is another good reason for us to under-take this program."

The objections of the other members of the group were violent indeed. "Preposterous" and "idiotic" and less printable characterizations flew back and forth across the conference table: "How can you think that they could absorb $20 billion a year—$600 a year per capita is several times as big as their total income right now. . . . $20 billion? That's more than total U.S. government nondefense pur-chases of goods and services by a wide margin. . . . Give that much to an unfriendly country? Never! ... You'll bankrupt us and cause a terrible inflation. ..."

Our friend listened quietly and waited for the excitement to die down before he began to speak again.

"I am surprised," he began, "that you should react this way when you have considered so many other radical and unconventional ideas in these meetings. On matters of government finance, however, it is clear that the conventional wisdom is extraordinarily tenacious. I think I had best begin, therefore, with a wise quotation from John Maynard Keynes, who said,

> It is curious how [we have] a preference for *wholly* "wasteful" forms of public expenditure rather than for *partly* "wasteful" forms, which, because they are not wholly wasteful, tend to be judged on strict "business" principles. ... Pyramid-building, earthquakes, even wars [and, if I may interject, even space programs and SSTs] may serve to increase wealth if the education of our statesmen on the principles of classical economics stands in the way of anything better.

"But, of course, I am talking about more than an enlightened fiscal policy. The important point is that Bwongwham, like many other underdeveloped countries, is seething with discontent; it is on the brink of social revolution, terrorism, and possibly civil war. In view of its strategic location and its independently minded communists, it is very much to our interest to see that no civil war does occur.

"If we do nothing, however, they *will* have a civil war. We will inevitably become involved, and in this world of ours, no involvements seem to be minor. I predict, in fact, that we will be spending this $20 billion a year on Bwongwham anyway—and their economy will 'absorb' it, all right, but in the form of homes, factories, and transport destroyed, not built. We will indeed send several hundred thousand American boys over there, but to kill, not to build.

"I do not question here the necessity of our becoming involved in this war if it occurs. What I do ask is this: Would you rather spend money avoiding a war or fighting it, *particularly while you still have the choice?*

"Can we 'afford' it? Can we 'afford' *not* to launch programs of this nature in view of the turmoil and impatience of poor people throughout the world? Indeed, we have tumultuous and impatient people at home as well, but our programs to overcome urban blight and lack of education, health, and opportunity are as piddling as our foreign-aid programs.

"Why is it that we appropriate for defense by the billions and then argue about the millions when it comes to programs to improve the quality of life? This year of 1964, the federal government will spend $50 billion on goods and services for defense and *less than one-third of that sum* on nondefense goods and services—that is what

I find incredible. Please let me stress again that the level of our defense expenditures may be unavoidably high, but I simply fail to understand the niggardliness in other areas; one is appropriated so readily, while the other is fought over line by line. It is a comfortable feeling to know you can blow anyone you want off the face of the earth, but I would like to think we were also bending maximum efforts to improve the face of the earth in the meantime—and if we fail to do so, we may have no choice but ultimately to start blowing it up.

"After all, after we have blown Bwongwham to bits, we'll have to spend more billions to rebuild it. Why not try to change the sequence just this one time?"

INDEX

Acquisitions. *See* Growth
　　companies
Active trading, 29
Affluence, 1, 122, 229, 238
Aggressive investing, 183, 192
American economy:
　　fundamental trends, 185
　　inflation and, 83
　　as inflation resistant, 234
　　strength of, 153, 164, 172
American Exchange, 43
American Stock Exchange:
　　characteristics of, 43
　　growth prospects,
　　　174–178
Asset management, 209.
　　See also Portfolio
　　management
Automation, 229, 241
Automobile industry, 59–60,
　　168, 231

Average daily volume,
　　1963–1969 figures,
　　176–177

Balance of payments:
　　crisis, 147, 149–153
　　gold and, 133–173
　　significance of, 50, 84,
　　　186–187
Baring Brothers, 150
Bastiat, Frederic, 164–165
Bearish market, 37, 171
Bear market:
　　characteristics of, 9,
　　　30–34, 41
　　duration of, 49
　　historical, 31–32
　　1967–1968, 42
　　in 1969, 200, 209
　　projections, 175
　　recovery from, 34–35

Bid, 32

Birth rates, 228

Blue chip stocks, 21–23, 25, 28–29, 33, 277

Bond market, 50, 114–118, 187–192, 206, 210

Bond portfolio, management of, 192–193

Book value, 68, 276

"Boom and bust" market, 41

British sterling, 47, 138, 161

Bull markets:
    characteristics of, 9, 17
    duration of, 49
    long-term, 202
    of 1949, 188
    projections, 176–177

Bullish market, 37, 50, 171

Burns, Arthur, 132

Business environment:
    dynamic, 267
    social change and, 248–255

Business expansion, 34, 54, 60–61

Business investment, 229–230

Buy-and-hold investments, 28, 41

Capital gains, 4–5, 12–13, 197, 208, 222–223, 279

Capitalism, 169, 255

Cash:
    accumulation, 32
    reserves, 181

Central bank, 162, 265–266

Commercial banks, loans from, 116, 129

Common Market, 153, 164–169

Commodity markets:
    impact of budget deficit, 163
    wheat, 149–151
    see also Gold

Common stock:
    acquisition transactions, 258–259
    government-issued, 275–278
    investing, 187–189, 191–193, 196–197, 206–210. See also Portfolio management; Stock market
    life-insurance purchases, 206–207
    liquidation of, 196–197
    pension-fund investments, 206
    risk and, 219–220
    shortage of, 200–202, 212

Conglomerates:
    acquisitions, 256–258
    management of, 259–261
    mergers, 257–258
    security packages, 258–259
    tender offers, 261

Consumer Price Index, 145

Consumer spending, 15–16, 120–121, 229, 236, 239–240

Convertible bonds, 193,
    200–201, 258, 279
Corporate stock ownership,
    net increase in, 202–203
Cost of living. *See* Inflation
Currencies, *see* British pound
    sterling; Dollar; Gold

Debt:
    corporate, 198–199, 202
    cost of, 199–200
Declining markets, 36–37. *See
    also* Bearish market; Bear
    markets
Defense establishment, 6
Defensive common stock, 220
Defensive investing, 183
Deflation, 86, 105, 117, 146,
    235, 267
Depreciation, 199
Depression, 121
Devaluation, 154–164
Dividends, 65, 67–68, 70,
    77, 79, 199, 258–259,
    276, 278
Dollar:
    budget deficits, 162–163
    devaluation of, 116, 113,
        146, 154–164, 169–172
    gold and, 134–136, 146–
        147, 157–158, 170–171
    protection strategies,
        148–149
    psychological influences on,
        158–160

strength of, 169–173
suspension of convertibility
    into gold, 158, 160,
    162, 173
value of, historical, 45
Dow Jones Industrial Average,
    12, 15, 33, 37, 67–68,
    70–71, 78–79
Down markets, 188
Downtrends, 20
"Dynamic" stock, 63

Economic expansion, 150
Economic Man (Adam
    Smith), 27
Employment, *see*
    Unemployment
    need for, 239–248
    rate, influential factors,
        167–168, 226
Equanimity, 14
Equity financing, 199–201
Equity investments, 196–202,
    204–212
Estate taxes, 208
Exports. *See* Balance of
    payments

Federal Reserve:
    functions of, 117
    gold prices, 172
    monetary policy, 124–125
    powers of, 157
Federal Reserve Bank of
    New York, 137

Fiscal policy, 50, 164, 232, 234–236, 282

Fixed-income securities, 184, 191, 194, 220

Flat trends, 205, 207

Forecasting, 9–10, 40–44

Foreign exchange:
markets, 157. *See also* Balance of payments
rates, 170
reserves, 159

Foreign policy, 6

Foreign trade, 45–46, 49

Free-enterprise system, 28, 255, 261

Free market, 122–123

French franc, 172–173

Fundamentals, 32

Galbraith, John Kenneth, Fulbright hearings testimony, 11–14, 250

Gift tax, 208

Gold:
balance of payments and, 133–173
convertibility of dollars into, 158, 160, 162, 173
demonetization of, 272–273
devaluation of dollar and, 150, 154–156, 170–171
discovery of, 140–141
foreign purchase of, 137–138, 172–173, 264–265

hoarding of, 171–173, 268
mining, 141–142, 270–271
as monetary standard, 138–139, 265–269
orthodox view of, 262–263
outflow of, 150–151
price of, 269–270
public attitude towards, 146
reserve, 147, 159
securities markets and, 44–51
significance of, 139–140, 142–143
speculation in, 143–149, 171
value of, 135–136, 265

Government:
budget deficit, impact of, 161–163
business decisions and, 250–251
capital markets, impact on, 4
common stock issues, 275–278
defense expenditures, 6–7
devaluation of dollar, 160–161
federal budget, 234
finance, 281–282
inflation and, 84, 118–132, 168
pork barrel legislation, 150
spending, *see* Government spending

surplus, 4–5
social change and, 251–252
Government spending:
    defense expenditures, 253,
        283–284
    frightening of businessman
        by, 253–254
    increase in, 233
    as inflationary, 235
    nondefense expenditures,
        233–234
    reduction in, 232–233
    significance of, 225–226
Great Depression, 59, 252
Gross national product
    (GNP), 105, 172, 226,
    231–232, 253
Growth companies:
    business expansion and,
        60–61
    characteristics of, 53–57
    comparison of, 69–81
    defined, 52
    earnings, 65–68, 70,
        72–74, 81
    listing of, 64–66, 70
    market development, 59
    qualitative analysis, 69–70,
        73, 78–79
    qualitative requirements,
        66–67
    trends in, 62–63
Growth stocks:
    characteristics of, 10, 219
    growth companies *vs.,* 51–81

Housing, 122

Imports. *See* Balance of
    payments
Income, personal, 241–244
"Incomes policy," 120. *See also*
    Inflation
Income stocks, 278–279
Individual investors:
    characteristics of, 25
    common stock portfolios,
        208–210
    liquidation, 210–211
Inflation:
    causality, 85
    characteristics of American
        economy, 83, 186
    deficits, relationship with,
        91–96
    devaluation and, 157
    expectation of, 124–125,
        131–132
    gold profit and, 156
    government spending and,
        234–235
    hedges against, 108,
        130–132, 170, 209–210
    impact of, 86–91, 187
    resource allocation,
        123–125
    stock market myths,
        96–103
    taxation and, 108–113
Inflationary mentality, 123,
    125–129

Inflationary pressures, 210
Inflationary spiral, 268
"Instant performance" fad, 24
Institutional investors,
    projections for, 204
Institutional trading:
    mutual funds, 26–27
    portfolios, trends in,
        20–25, 180
    turnover rates, 43–44
Interest rates:
    corporate debt, 198–201
    gold and, 48
    impact of inflation, 121–122
    influential factors, 193
    long-term, 50, 118
    short-term, 118
    stock market and, 33, 50
International financial
    system, 172
International Monetary Fund
    (IMF), 159, 269
International monetary
    system, 48–49, 113–114,
    136, 138
Investor psychology, 50, 192.
    See also Inflationary
    mentality

Kennedy, John F., 135–136, 169
Keynes, Lord John Maynard,
    17, 20, 143, 249, 268,
    282
Korean War, economic impact
    of, 124

Labor force:
    increase in, 231, 235, 237,
        245–246
    implications of, 128, 145
    shortage of, 228
    women in, 245–246
Law of Comparative
    Advantage, 153
Leisure time, 246–247
Liquidation, 181–182, 188,
    196, 205, 208–210, 218
Liquidity, 126–127, 198–199,
    202, 269
Loans, inflation and, 129–130

Margin requirements, 12–13
Market bottoms, bear markets,
    30–31
Market price, 70, 73
Market value, 22–23, 70, 211
Marshall Plan, 133
Merger exchanges, 201
Mergers, 257–258
Minnesota Mining and
    Manufacturing (3M), 62
Monetary barriers,
    268–269
Monetary policy, 124–125,
    146, 163
Money:
    in circulation, 150
    as medium of exchange,
        271–272
    professional management,
        210–211

Index

Money supply:
   government influence on,
      162–163
   implications of, 126,
      266–267
   increase in, 157
Monopolies, 257
Moody's industrial
      average, 67
Mortgages, 3–4
Mutual funds, 26–27, 38, 42,
      207, 210

Neill, Humphrey, 227, 231
New York Stock Exchange,
      9–10, 26, 29, 36, 40–44,
      174, 196, 200
Nongrowth stocks, 79

Oligopolistic markets, 168
Open market debt
      securities, 210
Options, 200
"Out of the market," 201
Over-the-counter stocks, 43
Overvalued stock, 79–80

Pension-fund investing, 26,
      28–29, 42, 183–195
Portfolio management:
   aggressive, 192
   conservative, 215–216
   defined, 194
   institutional, 20–25,
      180–181, 207–208

investment objective,
      217–218, 224
investment policy, 187
losses, 182
pension-fund investing,
      183–195
portfolio planning,
      218–221
risk management, 180–183,
      194–195, 212–216
staying-power, 181–182
success factors, 185,
      195–197
tax switching, 222–224
Poverty, 246, 249
Preferred bonds, 258
Price control, 126, 129–132.
      See also Inflation
Price/earnings ratio, 72, 76
Price/earnings-increase ratio,
      75–78, 81
Private sector, incomes of, 230
Productivity, influential
      factors, 123, 126–129,
      152–153, 229, 234, 241,
      246–247
Public sector, 230, 237
Public trading, 43

Real estate investments,
      206, 210
Recessions, 39, 128, 175
Retirement, early, 231
Risk exposure, 192. *See also*
      Risk management

Risk management, 180–183, 212–216
"Run on the bank," 158, 160, 162

Selling pressure, 32–33
Silver, as monetary standard, 138
Smith, Adam, 27, 168
Social balance, 250
Soft currency, 148
"Sour hedge," 118
Soviet Union, economic goals of, 254–255
Special Drawing Rights, 263
Speculation, 12, 20–25, 46–47
Stagnation, 197, 202
Standard & Poor's:
  500 index, 7, 19–20
  industrial-stock average, 34
Standard of living, 239–244, 253
Stearns, Linhart, 227
Steel industry, 55–57
Stock market:
  break of 1962, 135
  crash of 1929, 9, 12, 31
  forecasting, 9–10, 40–44
  Fulbright's hearings, 8–9, 10–16
  historical performance, 8–9, 17, 105–106
  inflation and, 84–85, 118
  in 1950s, 28–29
  speculation, 12, 20–25

trends, 16, 17, 19–20, 26
turnover rates, 36–39, 41–42
volume, 24, 35–40
see Bear markets; Bull markets
Stock selection, 73
Stock splits, 65
Supply and demand, 123–132, 212, 229–230, 235
Swiss francs, 170

Tariffs, Common Market, 167–169. See also Taxation
Taxation:
  capital gains, 12, 222–223
  government cuts in, 162–163, 232–233
  income redistribution, 243–244
  income tax surcharge, 5, 114, 119, 126
  inflation and, 119, 121–122
  liquidation and, 208–209
Tax-exempt bonds, 219
Technological change, 229
Tender offers, 261
Trading activity, 1966 figures, 21
Trading range, 35
Turnover rate, 43–44, 178, 207

Underdeveloped countries, 280–284

Index

Undervalued stocks, 76, 79
Unemployment:
    future of, 249
    impact of, 229–232,
        235–236
    inflation and, 106–107, 119,
        123, 127–128
    voluntary, 247
United States Savings
    Bonds, 207
Uptrends, 16, 17, 19–20,
    39–40, 63, 189
Utility stocks, 28

Valuation, 10
Vietnam War, economic
    impact, 46, 117, 124,
    185–187
Volume, in stock market, 24,
    35–40, 118

Wage:
    contracts, 127
    rates, 229–230
Wage-price spiral,
    143–145, 158
War, inflation and, 235
Warrants, 258, 279
Waste, public and private,
    282
Wealth distribution, 253
Whipsaw, 34
Working capital, 198
World War II:
    impact on stock market, 17
    postwar stock prices, 31

Yield, on bonds, 191,
    193–194

Zero growth, 128–129